Biopiracy: International Perspective and the Case of Ethiopia

Dagnachew Melese Tefera

Biopiracy: International Perspective and the Case of Ethiopia

Biopiracy and the case of 'Teff'

LAP LAMBERT Academic Publishing

Impressum / Imprint

Bibliografische Information der Deutschen Nationalbibliothek: Die Deutsche Nationalbibliothek verzeichnet diese Publikation in der Deutschen Nationalbibliografie; detaillierte bibliografische Daten sind im Internet über http://dnb.d-nb.de abrufbar.
Alle in diesem Buch genannten Marken und Produktnamen unterliegen warenzeichen-, marken- oder patentrechtlichem Schutz bzw. sind Warenzeichen oder eingetragene Warenzeichen der jeweiligen Inhaber. Die Wiedergabe von Marken, Produktnamen, Gebrauchsnamen, Handelsnamen, Warenbezeichnungen u.s.w. in diesem Werk berechtigt auch ohne besondere Kennzeichnung nicht zu der Annahme, dass solche Namen im Sinne der Warenzeichen- und Markenschutzgesetzgebung als frei zu betrachten wären und daher von jedermann benutzt werden dürften.

Bibliographic information published by the Deutsche Nationalbibliothek: The Deutsche Nationalbibliothek lists this publication in the Deutsche Nationalbibliografie; detailed bibliographic data are available in the Internet at http://dnb.d-nb.de.
Any brand names and product names mentioned in this book are subject to trademark, brand or patent protection and are trademarks or registered trademarks of their respective holders. The use of brand names, product names, common names, trade names, product descriptions etc. even without a particular marking in this work is in no way to be construed to mean that such names may be regarded as unrestricted in respect of trademark and brand protection legislation and could thus be used by anyone.

Coverbild / Cover image: www.ingimage.com

Verlag / Publisher:
LAP LAMBERT Academic Publishing
ist ein Imprint der / is a trademark of
OmniScriptum GmbH & Co. KG
Heinrich-Böcking-Str. 6-8, 66121 Saarbrücken, Deutschland / Germany
Email: info@lap-publishing.com

Herstellung: siehe letzte Seite /
Printed at: see last page
ISBN: 978-3-659-66229-4

Dagnachew M. Tefera
Biopiracy: International Perspective and the Case of Ethiopia

Table of Contents

ACKNOWLEDGEMENT..6

ACRONYMS 7

ABSTRACT...9

CHAPTER ONE 11

1.INTRODUCTION 11
1.1.Background... 11
1.2. STATEMENT OF THE PROBLEM 14
1.3. RESEARCH QUESTIONS.. 15
1.4. OBJECTIVES OF THE STUDY 15
1.5. SIGNIFICANCE OF THE STUDY 16
1.6. SCOPE OF THE STUDY 17
1.7. METHODOLOGY 17
1.8. LIMITATIONS OF THE STUDY 18
1.9. ORGANIZATION OF THE PAPER... 18

CHAPTER TWO 20

2. THE CONCEPT OF BIO-PIRACY.. 20
2.1. Patenting over biological resources (historical development) an Introduction 20
  2.1.1. The debate.. 27
  2.1.2. Patentability of Genetic Resources and Bio-piracy 28
  2.1.3. Criteria of patentability... 33
  2.1.4. Some examples of bio-piracy.. 35
  2.1.5. Patent as an instrument of stimulating and rewarding 37
2.2. BIO-PROSPECTING.. 41
2.3. INTERNATIONAL LEGAL INSTRUMENTS... 43
  2.3.1. Convention on Biological Diversity (CBD) 43
    2.3.1.1. Access and benefit sharing... 45
    2.3.1.2. Traditional knowledge 48

2.3.2. The Bonn Guideline (BGL) 50

2.3.3. The TRIPs and CBD; Interface... 55

2.3.3.1. TRIPs and Article 27.3 (b).. 55

2.3.3.2. TRIPs and CBD; Conflict or Coexist?... 59

2.3.3.3. The Disclosure Requirement.. 61

2.3.4. The Nagoya Protocol 64

2.3.4.1. Objectives of the Protocol... 65

2.3.4.2. An overview of the core provisions of the Nagoya provisions A) The preamble
.... 66

2.3.4.2.1. Achievements of the protocol 71

2.3.4.3. Nagoya Protocol and the Disclosure Requirement 75

CHAPTER THREE.. 77

3. THE ACCESS AND BENEFIT SHARING (ABS) REGIME OF ETHIOPIA 77

3.1. Introduction.. 77

3.2. The case of 'Teff'; a Breif story and Stutus quo.. 78

3.3. Patentability under the Ethiopian law and the TRIPs 87

3.4. Access and Benefit Sharing Regime of Ethiopia... 89

3.4.1. Proclamation No. 482/2006; A Proclamation to provide for Access to Genetic
Resources and Community Knowledge, and Community Right 90

3.4.1.1. The Preamble 90

3.4.1.2. General provisions Objectives of the proclamation.. 91

3.4.1.2.1. Ownership of genetic resources and community knowledge 92

3.4.1.2.2. Conditions of Access 93

3.4.1.2.3. Basic pre-conditions of permit.. 95

3.4.1.2.4. Special Access Permit... 97

3.4.1.2.5. Denial of Access 97

3.4.1.3. Access to Community Knowledge... 98

3.4.1.3.1. Access procedures.. 99

3.4.1.4. Benefit Sharing 100

3.4.1.5. Benefit sharing of local communities 101

3.4.1.6. Institutional Regime of ABS.. 101

3.4.1.7. Penalty... 104

3.5. The Ethiopian Legal Regime as compared to the Nagoya Protocol 106

CHAPTER FOUR.. **108**

4. CONCLUSION AND RECOMMENDATION 108

4.1. The Importance of Nagoya Protocol.. 111

4.2. Failures of the Protocol.. 112

4.3. Does Ethiopia benefit from NP? 113

4.4. Is our system (legal & institutional) well regulated to fight bio-piracy? 115

    4.4.1. Model Agreement on Access and Benefit Sharing of Genetic Resources of Ethiopia
.... 115

4.5. Recommendations.. 116

    4.5.1. Institutional amendments 123

BIBLIOGRAPHY **126**

ANNEX 1 .... **133**

Acknowledgement

First of all and above all I would like to give praise to my God for the unfinished love of Him on me. Thank you God for you have been my provider, guidance, and strength trough out my life and in this career as well. Yes you are my King indeed!

I would like to extend my heartfelt gratitude to my parents (Melese Tefera and Ejigayehu Lema) and also my sisters and brothers (Solomon, Yayneabeba, Embassy, and Kaleab) for their relentless prayer, support and encouragement; God bless you all!

My special thanks also go to my lovely fiancée (Zebib Getachew). I am privileged to have you in my life. Thank you honey for your prayer, encouragement and companionship in the process.

I would also like to thank the Institute of Biodiversity and Conservation for their cooperation in the processes of conducting this research work.

I am also indebted to the support of all my friends whose names are not listed here but whose contributions means a lot for the better accomplishment of my work. Many thanks friends!

Acronyms

ABS   Access and Benefit Sharing

BGL   Bon Guideline

CBD   Convention on Biological Diversity

CK   Community Knowledge

COP   Conference of Parties

DCs   Developing Countries

GATT General Agreement on Tariff and Trade

GRs   Genetic Resources

IP   Intellectual Property

IPR   Intellectual Property Right

MATs Mutually Agreed Terms

NGO   Non Governmental Organization

NP   Nagoya Protocol

PIC   Prior Informed Consent

PVP   Plant Variety Protection

TK   Traditional Knowledge

TKUP Traditional Knowledge of the Use of Plants

TRIPS Trade Related Intellectual Property Rights

UN   United Nations

UNCED The United Nations Conference on Environment and Development

UNEP United Nations Environment Program

UPOV Union pour la Protection des Obstentions Vegetales

USPTO   United States Patent and Trademark Office

WTO   World Trade Organization

Abstract

All living organisms; plants, animals and microbes, carry genetic material that could be potentially useful to humans. These resources can be taken from the wild, domesticated or cultivated. There are significant potential benefits to be gained by accessing genetic resources and making use of them. They provide a crucial source of information to better understand the natural world and can be used to develop a wide range of products and services for human benefit. These include products such as medicines and cosmetics, as well as agricultural and environmental practices and techniques.

Hence the issue of ownership over genetic resources and related traditional knowledge has become one of the most controversial worldwide issues. The controversy is mainly between the developed and big international pharmaceuticals on the one hand and the bio-diverse countries, which in most cases are developing countries. There are two major lines of arguments; the first one is the common heritage argument which proposes that biological and genetic resources are common heritages of mankind; hence there should be no restriction of ownership. The second line of argument, however, recognizes the sovereign right and ownership of states over their genetic resources, hence, without their permission no one can either access or own their resources.

However, until 1990's there have been acts of accessing and owning the genetic resources and related traditional knowledge without the consent and/or permission of the owning state of the resource. It is this act of plunder of genetic resources that is depicted as an act of Bio -piracy. This free access regime was finally changed when the CBD was enacted in 1992 which intended to curb alarming rates of biodiversity loss and ensure that the discrepancy between resource provider and the technology developer became more balanced.

One of the agenda which further triggered the debate over ownership of genetic resources is the issue of patenting of life forms. The TRIPS one of the agreements developed by WTO to outline trade related intellectual property rights requires member states to grant patents for any invention, both for products and processes, in all technology fields without discrimination that is, including innovations

9

conducted in relation to genetic resources, subject to standard requirements, including the requirements that the invention be novel and industrially applicable.

The global north are for the patenting of life forms; because they claim that, it is an incentive for the innovations related with genetic resources. The global south on the contrary claim that; patenting is simply a mechanism developed by the industrially developed ones' to get access, monopolize and get the right of private ownership over our genetic resources and related knowledge. In other words, the later claim that it is a systematic act of Bio-piracy.

Many efforts have been made to settle this global issue. Among efforts made so far the Nagoya Protocol on Access to Genetic Resources and the Fair and Equitable Sharing of Benefits Arising from their Utilization is the most important and most recent. Its main aim is to ensure a fair and equitable sharing of benefits and providing internationally binding guideline on the issue. Our country Ethiopia has also encountered acts of bio-piracy over its endemic genetic/biological resources. In one way or another, the act of piracy starts and rests on access of genetic resources and benefit sharing as well. The act of improper access/plunder over our genetic resource 'Teff', which is also addressed by this work, is a recent and an ongoing phenomenon.

Hence, this work seeks to put light on the international debate revolving around ownership and patenting over genetic resources and making a close scrutiny on the Ethiopian legal system. It specifically tries to assess how prudent enough our legal regulation (legal and institutional) is, find the lope wholes that could possibly make us vulnerable and what legal and institutional amendments should be made to our legal system with a special reference to the Nagoya Protocol.

This study concludes that most of the provisions of the Ethiopian legal system on Access and Benefit Sharing are mostly similar with the recently developed international guidelines and conventions. This however, does not mean that our legal system is regulated well enough without leaving any room for any acts of piracy. Especially in line of the most recent protocol (Nagoya Protocol) and experience of other countries; there should be some amendments, introduction of new provision and institutional amendments as well that the researcher recommends.

Chapter One

1. Introduction

1.1. Background

Genetic resources were considered as the **'common heritage of mankind'** and as a result they were treated as freely accessible commodities.[1] However, currently, there is a move towards ownership on biological/genetic resources. Biological diversities/genetic resources are important for the life of human being on earth and are one of the pillar sources of sustainable development and food security for the world as a whole.

One bio-prospecting firm defines biodiversity as the total variety of life on earth, including genes, species, and ecosystems and the complex interactions among them. For example, biodiversity samples can be collected from "geothermal and hydrothermal vents, acidic soils and boiling mud pots, alkaline springs, marine and freshwater sediments, marine symbionts, manure piles, contaminated industrial sites, arctictundra, dry Antarctic valleys, super cooled sea ice, microbial mats, bacterial communities associated with insects and nematodes, and fungi and plant endophytes.[2]

Article two of the CBD[3] defines the term biological diversity in its broader sense. The biological diversity may include all ecosystem, plant and animal species, and genetic resources. The biological diversity is also important for evolution and maintaining sustainable life system of the biosphere. Biological resources are vital for humanity's survival and for the economic and social development of nations. However, biological diversity is under threat around the

---

[1] P. Oldham, Global Status and Trends in Intellectual Property Claims: Genomics, Proteomics and Biotechnology ,(2004), UNEP/CBD/WG-ABS/3/INF/4

[2] P. Pan, Bio-prospecting: Issues and Policy Considerations,(2006), Honolulu, Legislative Reference Bureau, p4

[3] The CBD is a convention adopted during the Rio Earth Summit in 1992 under the auspices of the United Nations. The convention came in to force 1993 having three main objectives: the conservation, sustainable use of biological diversity and benefit sharing of genetic resources. The CBD is a legally binding framework for the conservation and sustainable use of all biological diversity and is intended to establish processes for the equitable sharing of benefits arising from the use of biodiversity.

world.

Ecosystems are being damaged or destroyed and species are disappearing. The global scale of biodiversity loss demands concerted international action. The issue of bio piracy is a world agenda in relation to the need to protect bio-diversity. Developed countries and companies are exploiting genetic resources and traditional knowledge of other countries', mostly of the un-industrialized and bio diversified countries', for commercial purpose without the informed consent or permission of those countries of origin. Such acts in effect will lead to over exploitation of genetic resources and endanger the bio diversity of the world as a whole and the benefit of the country or community of origin. The international framework for concerted action of bio diversity protection is the **United Nations Convention on Biological Diversity (CBD).**

This convention and other related international instruments are also concerned with traditional knowledge of a community.

On the other hand, one of the agreements in the rounds of negotiations under the WTO is the TRIPS agreement. It mainly deals with trade related intellectual property rights. Among which article 27.3 (b) provides that countries should provide either a patent or an effective form of sui-generis for the protection of plant varieties and micro organisms. This has created a great controversy between the technology reach and resource rich countries.

This patenting regime of the TRIPS agreement is also considered as one form of bio-piracy. There is growing worldwide opposition to the granting of patents on biological materials such as genes, plants, animals and humans. Farmers and indigenous peoples are outraged that plants that they developed are being 'hijacked' by companies. Groups as diverse as religious leaders, parliamentarians and environment NGOs are intensifying their campaign against corporate patenting of living things.

Developing countries rich in biodiversity, local communities and indigenous peoples, have been long struggling to establish ownership and maintain sovereign control over their genetic resources and traditional knowledge to protect them from misappropriation and unfair exploitation, particularly by foreign biotechnology-based industries. These developing countries consider that the current intellectual property system does not serve their interests in this respect, and thus call for changes both within and outside the intellectual property system.

The quest to solve the problem of bio-piracy was one of the legacies of the UN Convention on Biological Diversity, agreed at Rio in 1992. This states as one of its objectives the "fair and equitable sharing of benefits arising from the utilization of genetic resources" – but it took another 18 years to reach agreement on how to do this.

The breakthrough came in October 2010 at the UN Biodiversity Summit in Nagoya, Japan, when international negotiators reached a last-minute agreement on the wording of the protocol. The effect of the Nagoya Protocol is to outlaw bio-piracy by providing a legally binding framework and code of conduct for the sourcing and use of genetic material. Importantly, the protocol also places the traditional knowledge and medicines of indigenous people and local communities on a par with the natural resources themselves - requiring that this knowledge can only be used if informed consent is obtained in advance and the benefits are shared. It aims to stop 'bio-piracy', the theft of genetic resources and traditional knowledge in relation to genetic resources. The fact that countries like USA and Australia, greater consumers of bio-diversity resources, didn't sign the protocol makes the issue of bio-piracy more complicated and hot world agenda.

The purpose of this paper is, hence, to critically analyze the above mentioned and other relevant international instruments, policies and international debates in relation to bio-piracy. Currently the Nagoya Protocol is going under the process of becoming law and in February over one hundred countries are expected to sign up to the Nagoya Protocol. Therefore, this paper will also make a special emphasis to this protocol and will also try to incorporate recent developments which will come into being after the summit in February.

Our country Ethiopia; first is in the process of accession to the WTO, which is in effect to the TRIPS too in which case a patent regime compatible with the

13

TRIPS agreement is required. Second, Ethiopia is one of the states with diverse genetic resources and traditional knowledge. Hence, there is an eminent danger of bio-piracy. There have been cases in relation to bio-piracy, some of which are even not yet resolved. As a result Ethiopia has enacted two legislations in 2006.

This paper will try to give a vivid picture of the legal and institutional regime of our legal system and also makes a closer scrutiny to the existing legal and institutional regimes in light of their relevance in fighting bio-piracy against the genetic resources of the country and traditional knowledge of the community.

1.2. Statement of the problem

This patenting regime of the TRIPS agreement is also contested as one form of bio-piracy. There is growing worldwide opposition to the granting of patents on biological materials such as genes, plants, animals and humans. Farmers and indigenous peoples are outraged that plants that they developed are being 'hijacked' by companies. Groups as diverse as religious leaders, parliamentarians and environment NGOs are intensifying their campaign against corporate patenting of living things.

Developing countries rich in biodiversity, local communities and indigenous people, have been long struggling to establish ownership and maintain sovereign control over their genetic resources and traditional knowledge to protect them from misappropriation and unfair exploitation, particularly by foreign biotechnology-based industries. These developing countries consider that the current intellectual property system does not serve their interests in this respect, and thus call for changes both within and outside the intellectual property system.

As has been mentioned above in the background, in 2010 the Nagoya Protocol has been signed with aim of outlawing piracy activities made against natural resources.

Our country Ethiopia, first, is in the process of accession to the WTO, which is in effect to the TRIPS too; in which case a patent regime compatible with the

TRIPS agreement is required.[4]

Second, Ethiopia is one of the states with diverse genetic resources and traditional knowledge. Hence, there is an eminent danger of bio-piracy. There have been cases of bio-piracy, some of which are even not yet resolved. As a result Ethiopia has enacted two legislations in 2006. (Proclamations No. 482/2006 and Regulation No. 169/2009)

1.3. Research Questions

The research work, hence, will try to answer the following research questions.

What are the ongoing global debates related with bio-piracy side by side with the idea of patenting over genetic resources?

What are legal and institutional regulations of Ethiopia related with bio-piracy?

Is the Ethiopian legal regulation prudent enough in fighting up against piracies that could be made on our natural resources and traditional knowledge?

1.4. Objectives of the study

While the main targets of this research paper are to analyze the international debate and the possible outcomes/way forward of the issue of bio-piracy and evaluating how well regulated is our legal system in fighting bio-piracy; it also has the following specific objectives.

To analyze the relevant international legal instruments and policies related with bio-piracy; with a special emphasis to the Nagoya Protocol on ABS

---

[4] One of the provisions under the TRIPS agreement (Art. 27.3) requires member states to provide for a patenting regime for micro-organisms, and essentially biological processes for the production of plants or animals.

To critically analyze the treatments accorded to the issue of bio-piracy under each instrument.

Giving a clear picture about the legal and institutional regime of the Ethiopian legal system on biodiversity in general and with a specific emphasis to bio-piracy.

To check how well regulated (the legal and institutional aspect) in our legal system to fight piracies made on the genetic resources and related community knowledge of different societies.

And suggesting the way forward; the policy direction to be possibly followed internationally and the amendments that our legal system needs accordingly, if any.

1.5. Significance of the study

This research work is important in many aspects. Our country Ethiopia has applied for the membership of WTO in 2003 and going through the accession process since then. Upon accession one of the instruments that is expected to be signed is the TRIPS agreement. One of the controversial provisions of the TRIPS agreement is Art. 27.3 which requires members states to provide for a patent regime for micro-organisms, and essentially biological processes for the production of plants or animals and for plant varieties. And this is one of the controversial provisions that raised the issue of bio-piracy vs. patenting. Therefore, this paper is important in suggesting the kind of legal system that we should follow.

The requirements under different international legal instruments including the CBD and the TRIPS are minimum requirements or standards that should be followed by member states. As far as the member states' legislations are up to the standard; it is the individual states that regulate specific matters. In fighting against bio-piracy, hence, what matters is 'how well regulated is the
domestic law?' Therefore, this work will be important in showing the potential risk areas, i.e. areas not well regulated, and in suggesting the kind of precocious

16

measures and legislative amendments that should be made if any.

1.6. Scope of the study

The study taking general issues of biodiversity as a background; it will focus only in the area of and issues related with bio-piracy. In doing so; it will make reference only to the relevant international legal instruments and to domestic laws of Ethiopia. Moreover, it discusses only the legal and institutional regimes of our law (Proclamation No.482/2006, Proclamation No.123/1995, and Reg. No. 169/2009)

1.7. Methodology

This research is a doctrinal research and has employed a combination of several approaches. The researcher has conducted literature review, analysis of international and national legal instruments and discussions with authorities. Literature review has mainly provided for the conceptual frame work of bio-piracy and related or ongoing debates and perspectives. Discussion on bio-piracy presupposes issues related with access and benefit sharing of genetic resources and the patenting regime of intellectual property rights. The issue of bio-piracy and what this paper is all about revolves around these two issues; access and benefit sharing and patenting over genetic inventions.

In doing so analysis and explanation of the relevant legal regimes is made in conducting the research. The CBD (Convention on Biological Diversity) is the first international instrument recognizing states sovereign right over their biological resources and trying to regulate the issues of access and benefit sharing. The CBD has three main objectives; conservation of biodiversity, sustainable use of the components of biodiversity and facilitating access and equitable sharing of benefits arising from commercial utilization of genetic resources. In implementing the third objective the Bonn Guideline (2002) and the latest Nagoya Protocol has (2010) has been enacted consequently. Concerning issues of patenting the TRIPs agreement is the relevant instrument as it is the only internationally binding legal instrument requiring member states to provide for either a patent or an effective sui generis for

17

inventions in any field, with some exceptions and flexibilities, as far as the inventions fulfills criteria of patentability Therefore analysis and explanation on each of the above listed international instruments is employed while making a relevance references to the issue of bio-piracy.

Analysis of the Ethiopian law is also made relating with international instruments. The proclamation and regulation on access and benefit sharing have been discussed and analyzed thoroughly. As the paper tries to revise the ABS regulation of the country, whether it well regulated or not in fighting bio-piracy, a reference should be made to the relevant international instruments. And a special emphasis is made to the Nagoya Protocol as it the most detailed and recent instrument on ABS. In addition discussion with concerned authorities of Institute of Biodiversity and Conservation and Intellectual Property office has been made to gather additional information.

1.8. Limitations of the study

One of the major limitations to this work is lack of adequate literature and research works on the area of bio-piracy with emphasis to case of Ethiopia. The other is as domestic laws on the area of biodiversity, generally, are recent developments to our legal system; not well practiced and no well organized institutional establishment except the IP office.

1.9. Organization of the paper

This paper is comprised of four chapters. The first chapter is shows the proposal of this thesis. The second chapter, The Concept of Bio-piracy, tries to provide the lying grounds/basic ideas of bio-piracy and the debate among international groups internationally. The third chapter, Access and Benefit Sharing Regime of Ethiopia, explores international, local and regional legal instruments on access and benefit sharing and how the issue of access and benefit sharing is directly related with bio-piracy. And a brief discussion on the ABS regime of Ethiopia by comparing with other international ABS regimes is made with a special emphasis to the Nagoya Protocol. In the fourth chapter, the last chapter, the researcher gives conclusive

18

remarks and recommends the way forward/what should be done concerning our ABS regime so that it could best fight bio-piracy.

Chapter Two:

2. The Concept of Bio-piracy

2.1. Patenting over biological resources (historical development) an Introduction

Although the importance of plants to human civilization is well recognized, controversy surrounds the legal ownership and control of plant resources. The word bio-piracy and the context it refers to is not a phenomenon with a long legal and philosophical history/background. Issues of biodiversity, in general, and of bio-piracy specifically are current developments in the political, economic and social agendas of the world. As an effect of globalization and technological development issues of utilization, ownership, and conservation of natural resources, which used to be considered as common heritages, began to be one of the most controversial world agendas.

To worsen the case (the international controversy) consequently, many issues related with biodiversity, biotechnology and IPR started to emerge; bio-piracy is one.

Hence, defining the term and the idea of bio-piracy is not an easy task as there is no international consensus as to the working definition for the term bio-piracy and the concept of bio-piracy itself. Before, going through definitions given by different institutions, tribunals, scholars and international legal instruments let us first look on how the issue of bio-piracy emerged.

There is much tension today between the patent, the world's oldest regularly established intellectual property right, and the laws and sentiments that have clustered around an amorphous body of genetic resources in many developing countries which preceded the adoption of patent laws in many of those countries.[5]

---

[5] T. Toshiko (ed.), Patent Law and Theory, A Handbook of Contemporary Research,(2008), Edward Elgar Publishing Limited, UK, p 143

The issue of bio-piracy concerns law, ethics, morality, and fairness. There are different views as to the issue of bio-piracy and IPR/patentability as opposed to the right of indigenous people. [6]

In order to arrive at a definition of bio-piracy one must appreciate the historical context within which the term arose. First, Western intellectual property owners have often accused Third World states and economic actors of "pirating" or unlawfully "appropriating" the intellectual property rights of industrialized entities, especially patents and copyrights. In the wake of biotechnological inventions and the patenting by Western states and entities of indigenous peoples bio-cultural resources, obtained without their lawful informed consent, Third World States contend that industrialized states, business entities, and research institutions are "pirating" their biological re-sources. Therefore, the Third World applies the term "bio-piracy" to describe what it sees as a misappropriation of indigenous peoples' knowledge and bio-cultural resources, especially through the use of intellectual property mechanisms.

If the infringement of patents, copyrights, and trademarks constitutes intellectual piracy, then so does the failure to recognize and compensate indigenous and traditional peoples for the creations arising from their knowledge. Inherent to the bio-piracy rhetoric are the notions of un-authorized appropriation/theft of biological diversity and its associated traditional knowledge. [7]

---

[6] For instance on the one side, defenders of traditional knowledge object that it is sometimes made the subject of patent applications, with the threat that well-tried treatments may be monopolized by foreign corporations and the high probability that those communities which have created and transmitted traditional knowledge will receive nothing in return. On the other side, pharmaceutical companies and bio-prospectors forcefully deny that any wrongful monopolization will take place, since the fundamental requirements of patentability such as the requirement that an invention be novel and non-obvious and the defence of prior use will ensure that traditional practices may be maintained. Moreover, they add, the patent system provides an incentive that enables them to invest in the improvement of folk remedies, the isolation and purification of the active ingredients of plants and herbs and the publication, in the patent application, of valuable information that will increase understanding of how traditional medicines work, thereby saving life and enhancing its quality. Politicians are asked to side with the one camp. Id, p 144

[7] M. Ikechi, Global Bio-piracy: Patents, Plants, and Indigenous Knowledge (2006), University of British Colombia Press, Columbia, p 12

There are three main reinforcing factors or issues central to the issue of bio-piracy. The first is socio-cultural; the Europeans starting from the colonial era believed that the intellect of the non European people is inferior to those of the Europeans. Therefore, the traditional efforts of farmers and breeders in the improvement of plant genetic resources which they used and preserved for centuries in their farms are unworthy of legal protection. In other words, bio-piracy can be understood as part of the cultural war with non-Western peoples, cultures, and epistemological frameworks.

The second central factor to the issue of bio-piracy is how the powerful and industrialized states (States of the North) created international agricultural research centers and gene banks meant to gather huge quantity and quality of plant life forms and genetic resources of the bio-diverse and technologically poor states (States of the South). The very justification that is mentioned behind this "activity of theft" (as quoted by the States of the South other opponents of this activity) is the notion of "common heritage of mankind". Therefore, one of the activities mentioned as bio-piracy is this act of relocating the resource of the south without any remuneration with the justification of common heritage of mankind.

The third and the most controversial factor central to the issue of bio-piracy (the idea which will be given a detailed emphasis by this paper) is patenting of plants, related traditional knowledge and use of plant and genetic resources through one of the IP tools called the patent system. [8]

The patent is the primary IPR that is sought in the field of biotechnology because it is meant to be a right concerning innovations used in new or improved products or processes. Patents enable the holder to exclude imitators from marketing such inventions or processes for a specified time; in exchange, the holder is required to disclose the formula or idea behind the product or process. After a patent is granted, the owner has a monopoly over commercial exploitation of the invention for a limited period. The stated purpose of a patent is to stimulate

---

[8] Id., pp 87-88

22

innovation by offering higher monetary returns than the market otherwise might provide. There are two problems that patent protection generates. The first concerns the monopolistic feature of the cost analysis of patent protection in this field. The classical IP scholarship has crafted each protection according to the principle of "allocative efficiency" according to which the long-term benefits flowing to society from the protection granted to a particular class of creators or innovators outweigh the (mainly short-term) costs imposed by the monopolistic structure of the patent grant. This is referred as the utilitarian approach to intellectual property rights, in which incentives to create new inventions (patent) are balanced against the benefits of relatively unrestricted public access to and use of inventions after a reasonable period of time has passed.[9] And the "mainstream legal literature" has applied this standard principle from IP economics to the patenting of biotechnology as well.[10] The second problem is generated when formal, industrial, patentable knowledge builds upon prior art of informal TK which is in a quasi-commons regime.

When it comes to the benefit sharing of the profits arising from the exploitation of this knowledge at the international level these problems are amplified.[11]

A vivid example of benefit sharing illustrates the controversy of private property rights in GRs and TK held by indigenous groups. Imagine a plant that produces a natural sweetener and has been preserved for several millennia in a local farming micro-culture. This sweetener performs its sweetening function without negative dietary or health side effects. A foreign corporation comes along bio-prospecting and secures samples of the local sweetening plant, maps its genome, and then proceeds to genetically engineer a plant that yields sweetener with a potency tenfold that of the original. The corporation then patents the modified plant, and the world quickly forgets the original plant as the patented plant is markedly more productive. Consequently, through commercialization, all

---

[9] B. Claude and E. John, Biotechnology and the Patent System : Balancing Innovation and Property Rights, (2007), The AEI Press, Washington D.C., p24
[10] M. Ricolfi, "Biotechnology, Patents and Epistemic Approaches" Journal of Biolaw &Business, (2002), Special Supplement, pp 77–90.

[11] C. Jonathan, The Protection of Biodiversity and Traditional Knowledge in International Law of Intellectual Property, (2010), Cambridge University Press, New York, pp 5-6

of the profits flow to the company patent holder without a farthing going to the indigenous farmers who preserved the plant for millennia. Some 6.5 percent of all genetic research undertaken in agriculture focuses on germ plasma derived from wild species and land races (farmer-developed varieties of crop plants that are adapted to local environmental conditions). Thus, the question is posed: is it fair to give the entire pastry to the one who adds the final cherry to the pie?[12]

This above mentioned approach is what is mostly quoted as bio-piracy. The term is not as such a legal term, let alone technical intellectual property terms. It, more of, has a political and sociological sense.

The term bio-piracy was coined by Mooney as part of a counter-attack strategy on behalf of DCs (Developing Countries) that, as already said, are accused by industrialized countries of supporting intellectual piracy, i.e., counterfeiting all types of goods protected in the industrialized countries by IPRs. In turn, DCs feel that they are no more pirates than corporations that acquire resources and TK from their countries, use them in their Research and Development programs, and acquire patents and other IPRs without compensating the provider countries and communities.[13]

Bio-piracy has emerged as a term to describe the ways that corporations from the developed world free-ride on the genetic resources, TK and technologies of developing countries. While these and other corporations complain about 'intellectual piracy' perpetrated by people in developing countries, the latter group of nations counters that their biological, scientific and cultural assets are being 'pirated' by these same businesses.[14]

Coming to the definition of the term; the word "bio-piracy" was coined to name a phenomenon that is not new but that has flourished under colonialism, capitalism

---

[12] Ibid

[13] Ibid

[14] T. Geoff and R. Tasmin (ed.), A Guide to International Negotiations and Rules on Intellectual Property, Biodiversity and Food Security (2008), Internal Development Research Center, Earthscan publisher, p147

and, more recently, globalization. By naming it, contemporary scholars have challenged a form of exploitation of peoples and of resources that now poses a threat to both cultural and environmental sustainability. The term "bio-piracy" is a direct challenge to the legitimacy of activities that have entered the mainstream of contemporary global capitalism.

According to the Concise Oxford Dictionary, 'piracy' means (1) the practice or an act of robbery of ships at sea; (2) a similar practice or act in other forms, especially hijacking; and (3) the infringement of copyright. Apart from the use of 'piracy' for rhetorical effect, the word does not seem to be applicable to the kinds of act referred to as bio-piracy. But what about the verb 'to pirate'? The two definitions given are (1) appropriate or reproduce (the work or ideas etc of another) without permission for one's own benefit; and (2) plunder.

These definitions seem to be more appropriate since inherent to the bio-piracy rhetoric are misappropriation and theft. In essence, 'bio-pirates' are those individuals and companies accused of one or both of the following acts: (1) the misappropriation of genetic resources and/or TK through the patent system and (2) the unauthorized collection for commercial ends of genetic resources and/or TK.[15]

Bio-piracy has been defined as 'appropriation of the knowledge and genetic resources of farming and indigenous communities by individuals or institutions seeking exclusive monopoly control (patents or intellectual property) over these resources and knowledge.[16]

It also refers to the use of intellectual property systems to legitimize the exclusive ownership and control over biological resources and biological products that have been used over centuries in non-industrialized countries and cultures.

Some other scholars and literatures use the term bio-piracy to depict bio-piracy as an unbalanced and non-reciprocal movement of plants and TKUP from the South to the North through the processes of international institutions and the patent

---

[15] Peter, cited above at note 2

[16] A definition by Vandana Shiva, a famous Indian scientist and activist

system. As Rosemary Coombe has rightly pointed out, this process is characterized by the non-recognition of the intellectual contributions of holders and practitioners of traditional knowledge towards the improvement of the plants or TKUP in question.[17]

A recent report on bio-piracy produced by the Edmonds Institute operated with a working definition of bio-piracy:

where there is access to or acquisition of bio-diversity (and/or related traditional knowledge) without prior informed consent, including prior informed consent about benefit sharing, on the part(s) of those whose biodiversity (or traditional knowledge) has been 'accessed' or 'acquired', there is bio-piracy i.e., theft.[18]

Ikechi Mgbeoji, in his book called, '*Global Bio-piracy: Patents, Plants, and Indigenous Knowledge*,' has given a more comprehensive definition for the term/the idea:-

Bio-piracy is the illegal appropriation of life—microorganisms, plants and animals (including humans)—and the traditional cultural knowledge that accompanies it. Bio-piracy is illegal because, in violation of inter-national conventions and (where these exist) corresponding domestic laws, it does not recognize, respect or adequately compensate the rightful owners of the life forms appropriated or the traditional knowledge related to their propagation, use and commercial benefit. Bio-piracy commonly operates through the application of Intellectual Property Rights (IPR) (primarily patents) to genetic resources and traditional knowledge[19]

2.1.1. The debate

---

[17] C. Rosemary, "The Recognition of Indigenous Peoples' and Community Traditional Knowledge in International Law" (2001) Thomas Law Review, vol. 14, p 285

[18] H. Chris, Biodiversity, Bio-piracy and Benefits: What allegations of Bio-piracy tell us about Intellectual Property, p 159, (unpublished)
[19] Mgbeoji, cited above at note 7, p1

There has also been a recent flurry of critiques of the notion of bio-piracy, claiming it as an alarmist exaggeration or a misguided reading of the nature of IPR law. For example, in a recent article, Chen claims that '[m]ost allegations of bio-piracy are so thoroughly riddled with inconsistencies and outright lies that the entire genre, pending further clarification, must be consigned to the realm of 'rural legend'[20]

Various factors have congregated to arouse a huge interest, indeed a controversy, with regard to the legal ownership of plant genetic resources and the knowledge associated with the uses of plants. This controversy has elicited calls for the creation of a regime dealing with access to and equitable sharing of the benefits of plant genetic resources. These issues are often conflated in what has become known as the issue of "indigenous people's knowledge."The debate has often implicated a variety of issues, such as the imposition of Eurocentric legal concepts (e.g., the imposition of patents on non-European cultures and peoples), the impact of globalization, and emerging norms on legal control of knowledge. In addition, the debate has raised issues pertaining to the prevailing ideology of "civilization" and "development" and its impact on biological and cultural diversity. At the heart of the debate is the political economy and legal control of plant genetic resources and knowledge of their associated uses. Often ignored in the discourse is the fact that the processes by which the dominant cultures and states appropriate the traditional knowledge of Third World peoples are masked in technical, and sometimes diplomatic, understatements. Consequently, it is often difficult to discern the issues at stake or the scale of the disagreements between those involved.[21]

The debate on ownership of plant genetic resources often extends to what may be called "traditional knowledge of the uses of plants," hereinafter referred to as TKUP. The definition of what constitutes TKUP is a little more problematic. TKUP is generally defined in very broad terms. It encompasses adverse range of tradition based innovations and creations arising from intellectual activity in the

---

[20] Hamilton, cited above at note 18, p 159

industrial, literary, or artistic fields of indigenous and traditional peoples. Its range includes agricultural products, the medicinal use of plants, and spiritual worldview. TKUP is not a monolithic entity; rather, it is diverse and sophisticated.[22]

2.1.2. Patentability of Genetic Resources and Bio-piracy

The field of biotechnology, though a recent global issue, is growing rapidly and is also advancing in the level of attention that the world politics, economy and socio-legal fields gives for the issue. The internationalization of the patent system, the international economics, and the rise of the biotechnology industry are some of the key issues which are related with and have an implication on bio-piracy.[23] Since the report of the first successful cloning of a sheep named Dolly in early 1997, advances in genetic engineering have gained attention on a global scale.[24]

In 1873, Louis Pasteur was granted a patent by the United States Patent and Trademark Office (USPTO), claiming 'yeast, free from organic germs of disease, as an article of manufacture'.[25]

The other famous case related with patenting of life forms and which marked the beginning of global attention to patentability of life forms is the American Supreme Court Case of Diamond v. Chakrabarty which happened in 1971.

In Chakrabarty, the court explicitly recognized the statutory right to patent life, overturning the long held precedent that excluded "product of nature" as patentable subject matter.[26]

In 1971, Indian microbiologist Ananda Mohan Chakrabarty, an employee of

---

[21] Mgbeoji, Cited above at note 7, p1

[22] Id, p 9

[23] Id., p 13

[24] Rowland A. et al, Patents and Biotechnology: Issues Around the Patenting of Life Forms

[25] Rimmer M., Intellectual Property and Biotechnology (2007), Edward Elgar Publishing Limited, UK, p 24

[26] David C.·"Traditional and Modern-Day Bio-piracy: Redefining the Bio-piracy Debate", J. ENVTL. LAW AND LITIGATION, [Vol. 19(2)], (2004), p 370

General Electric (GE), genetically engineered a form of bacteria that could break down crude oil; this bacterium could be used in the clean-up of oil spills. Soon thereafter, GE applied for a patent on Chakrabarty's genetically engineered oil-eating bacteria. The U.S. Patent and Trademark Office rejected GE's patent application, basing its decision on the traditional legal rule that "products of nature" (i.e., life forms) are not patentable subject matter under 35 U.S.C

The case was appealed all the way to the Supreme Court. In June 1980, by a five-to-four majority, the Court ruled that a patent should be granted to GE. In so holding, the Court implicitly reaffirmed its prior precedent which stated that "products of nature" could not be patented, and distinguished Chakrabarty's genetically-engineered bacteria on the basis that he had "produced a new bacterium with markedly different characteristics from any found in nature....." The Court elaborated, stating that "Chakrabarty's discovery is not nature's handiwork, but his own." In opening up an entirely new subject matter as patentable, the Chakrabarty decision had a profound effect on intellectual property law. In essence, the Chakrabarty decision created a slippery slope and paved the road for the expansion of patentability under section 101.[27]

In Diamond v. Chakrabarty case, the Court gave a green light to biotech researchers and investors by confirming that "life" can comprise patent-eligible subject matter.[28] In spite of the exclusion of plants and animals from patenting under U.S. law, the United States has since rushed to grant patents on all kinds of life-forms. Currently, well over 190 genetically engineered animals, including fish, cows, mice, and pigs, are figuratively standing in line to be patented by a variety of researchers and corporations.[29][30]

The very basic question at the heart of the issue is whether or not it is

---

[27] Ibid

[28] Margo A et al, "Patent First, Ask Question Later: Morality and Biotechnology in Patent Law", Mary Law Review, Issue 2 Volume 45 Article 3, (2003), pp485-486

[29] Shiva V., Bio-piracy: The plunder of Nature and Knowledge, (1997), South End Press, Brookline/USA, p27

[30] According to Kimbrell; the Supreme Court's Chakravarty decision has been extended to be paten to be continued, up the chain of life. The patenting of microbes has led inexorably to patenting of plants, and then animals. Ibid.

appropriate to grant patent protection for biotechnology inventions.[31] There are different arguments in favor and against patenting inventions related with life forms/genetic resources. There are also different philosophical justifications which work both for the IP system, generally, and for the patent protection system as well.

From the economic point of view; intellectual property, including patent, embody a balance between two extremes, each of which would hobble technological advancement.[32]

One of the extremes is that completely avoiding granting of any property right protection to inventors for their inventions. Sometimes, secrecy can provide reasonable protection against copying of inventions by competitors, but this is often impossible in industries where regulators and users of new technology require detailed information about the products they endorse or use.[33]

The other extreme would be to provide inventors with permanent protection against appropriation of their inventions by competitors. The profit/price that Patent and other IP protections set/generate is, mostly, well above marginal coast.[34] This "static inefficiency" would impede usage by buyers for whom the product is worth more than manufacturing and distribution costs but less than market prices. Perpetual patents would usually keep prices well above marginal costs until close substitutes could be brought to market, a process that might take many years. [35]

Patent and/or intellectual property protection as a whole is a tool internationally recognized in striking the balance between these two extremes; that is, first, inventors are granted patent rights for a limited period of time[36]; second, inventors are required to disclose publicly the essential of the inventions in the process of

---

[31] Rowland , cited above at note 24

[32] Barfield, cited above at note 9
[33] Ibid
[34] Id, p 26
[35] Ibid

[36] Recently set in the United States and other advanced nations at twenty years from the time a patent application is filed, Biotechnology and the patent system : balancing innovation and property rights, Ibid, p 25

granting patent. This greatly facilitates the development of competing products while contributing to advances in basic and applied science.[37]

Opposition to IP on ethical grounds arises largely arises from the concept of ownership over living products and life processes including the regeneration of life. These opponents note a fundamental difference from the transfer of ownership of seeds or specific animal breeds without any claim on their progeny.[38] This involves owning biomass only, and is a practice as old as commerce itself. The retention of tights over the regenerative capacity of organisms, while selling their biomass, is entirely new and extends ownership beyond society's accepted limits.

Opponents of patenting of living things morally object to the principle of intellectual property rights that privatize knowledge that they believe should be used for the good of all. Those who view bio-prospecting as bio-piracy view a potential remedy embodied in a certain global agreement as "an initiative of the North to globalize the control, management, and biological diversity of resources which lie primarily in the Third World." This view considers bio-prospecting as political, economic, and cultural oppression perpetrated by the money-rich, resource-poor north against the money-poor, resource-rich south. Furthermore, bio-piracy considers benefit-sharing agreements with host countries not worth the harm caused by bio-prospecting.[39]

Each step to recognize IPRs in plants and other life forms were faced with oppositions from different groups on various grounds that range from philosophical and moral arguments to social, environmental and economic reasons.[40]

---

[37] Ibid

[38] The Crucible Group, People ,Plants , and Patents: The impact of intellectual property on trade, plant, biodiversity, and rural society, (1994) , Published by the International Development Research Centre, Canada, , p 56

[39] Peter, cited above at note 2, p3

[40] Gizachew Sileshi, The Ethiopian Legal Regime on Plant Variety Protection: Assessment of Its Compatibility with TRIPs Agreement, Implications and the Way Forward, LL.M Thesis, AAU, Law Faculty,(2010), (Unpublished), P.1-2

Two events have changed the issue of patents and patentability of life forms and have transformed the patent into a critical issue that impinges upon the life of the common man. The first was a US Supreme Court decision to treat life as an invention and the second was the introduction of patents and intellectual property rights in the Uruguay Round of GATT by the influence of US.[41]

The early patent laws of the US used to grant patent protection for new inventions or new methods which were unknown in US, but practices anywhere else. Therefore, the main requirement is that it should be unknown and new only in US in order to get a patent protection.[42]

Hence, present day states of US started to enact laws which secure monopolies mostly based on imported technologies and methods of manufacture. The very justification was to encourage manufacturing thereby making the objective of patent protection promoting manufacturing than rewarding inventions.[43]

Article 27 of the WTO TRIPS agreement provides for the minimum standards that national member state's laws should include a patent system for genetic innovations.

The Trade Related Intellectual Property Rights (TRIPs) Agreement of GATT/WTO has globalized US style patent laws. This has far reaching consequences and impacts not only on our capacity to provide for our basic needs of food and medicine, but also on democracy and sovereignty. The universalization of patents to cover all subject matter, including life forms, has resulted in patents invading our forests and farms, our kitchens, and our medicinal plant gardens.

[41] Shiva V., Protect or Plunder? , Understanding Intellectual Property Rights,(2001) , Penguin Book India Ltd., India, p 1

[42] For example, if somebody in Europe were operation a machine and someone in the US independently and without knowledge of that existence in good faith developed his/her own invention, which was essentially the same machine, the fact that there is a similar machine which is already operating in Europe would not prevent him/her from obtaining a patent in the US. Protect plunder. The European invention would not be considered as prior art in US. Protect or Plunder?, Id, p17

[43] Gizachew Seleshi, cited above at note 40, p 17

Patents are now granted not just for machines but for life forms and biodiversity; not just for new inventions but for the knowledge of our grandmothers. Indigenous knowledge and hundreds of plants used in food and medicine are in imminent danger of being patented by the western world for commercial gain. This is tantamount to bio-piracy. [44]

For instance, prominent skeptics such as Pat Mooney of the Canadian activist group known as RAFI (Rural Advancement Foundation International) and the Indian eco-feminist Vandana Shiva and other groups argue that; TRIPs facilitates the piracy of indigenous knowledge. The problem is that TRIPs represents an alien jurisprudence. Indigenous peoples have their own normative structures governing the acquisition, transfer, and use of knowledge. To the extent that TRIPs does not recognize indigenous regimes, there is little question that it violates the equality and humanity of indigenous peoples across the world.

The question that arises now is how does the patent system appropriate genetic resources and traditional knowledge? Or how does the patenting system encourages bio-piracy?

To analyze how; we let us see some further issues of patentability and examples of bio-piracy.

2.1.3. Criteria of patentability

Historically, there are three different uses of patent; 'patents for conquests', 'patents for inventions' and 'patents for imports'. But the different functions of patents have never been neatly separated. [45]

In the beginning, patents referred to letters patent (a literal translation of the Latin litterae patents)). The adjective 'patent' means open, and originally patents referred to the 'letters patent' or open letters which were official documents by which certain privileges, rights, ranks or titles were conferred by sovereign rulers.

---

[44] Id. pp 3-4

[45] Id., p 11

They were 'open' because they were publicly announced and had a seal of the sovereign grantor. The 'openness' had nothing to do with disclosure of an invention as is commonly assumed in the present day context.[46]

Patentable subject matters were originally intended to be limited to machines, processes involving new art, composition of matters and design. Life forms, including plants, were excluded from patentability. Today, however, the scope of patentable subjects includes artificially modified life forms and DNA sequences. For an invention to be patentable it must be novel, must involve inventive step and utility of invention, industrial application. Same criteria are applied to grant patent for genetic related inventions. These requirements set the basic standards of patentability by ensuring that inventions were not previously available to the public; are sufficiently different from what was previously available to the public and are capable of industrial applicability.

Applying these criteria for patenting biological inventions creates many problems of compliance with the criteria. For instance concerning novelty it controversial what amounts to 'new'. It is difficult to explain or almost impossible to explain the complete description of the morphological characteristics and features such as **"the taste of a fruit, the smell of a flower**, the **baking power** of a cereal or the **brewing power** of barley" and is difficult to reduced to documentary specification capable of enabling a skilled person in the art to replicate the plant or the invention in consideration.[47] It was for this reason that classical patent theorists opined that, in the absence of radical legislative changes, the patent system could not be applied to plants. [48]

---

[46] Id., p 12

[47] Mgbeoji, Cited above at note 7, p 134

[48] Indeed, attempts to cure this juridical black hole by requiring the deposit of the "new" plant hardly ameliorate the radical defect in specifying the purported new plant. The major advantage in written specification is that it enables the public, with minimum hassle, to have access to the information contained in the disclosure. This need is hardly resolved by depositing the new plant with the patent office. It is difficult to conceive of how depositing a sample of the new plant could be of any scientific value to interested members of the public or how it would enable thousands of other persons skilled in the art in question to have easy access to what is meant to be a novel addition to knowledge in the public domain. In the Pioneer Hi-Bred case the Supreme Court of Canada considered the issue and reasoned that, since a specification. Ibid

Whether discovering a natural resource already existing but never known to the public before the filling date new or not. The major approach followed on this issue is either excluding naturally occurring things from patentability, since it is merely discovery which is not patentable, or putting requirement prior art that is the invention should be something not anticipated by a prior art or not known to the public before. Same approach is followed by our system.[49]

The other requirement is inventive step which requires that for a patent to be granted for an invention it should be inventive and non obvious to a person skilled in the art. It is obvious that a naturally occurring animal or plant cannot by itself have an inventive step unless some effort of human is added. It still difficult to define what constitutes an inventive step.[50]

2.1.4. Some examples of bio-piracy

Local farmers in Nigeria developed an insect-resistant cowpea. Needless to say, those local farmers did not "publish" their findings or their results in a "reputable journal" reviewed by their "peers." However, on a trip to West Africa, Angharad Gatehouse, a scientist at the University of Durban, obtained some of these seeds. Using "formal" techniques, he identified in "scientific language" the genetic mechanism that causes the locally developed cowpeas to be insect-resistant. As Buchanan notes, "he [the scientist] promptly left the university and joined Agricultural Genetic Company of Cambridge and they proceeded to apply for a patent on their 'invention.'" The practical result was that local farmers were short-changed by the inter-play of patent systems, which erased their hard work and intellect simply because they failed to "publish" their observations in written

---

[49] Proclamation Concerning Inventions, Minor Inventions and Industrial Designs, Proclamation NO.123/1995, Negarte Gazeta,54 The Year,no.25,Article, Article 3 (2) (hereinafter Proclamation 123/1995)
[50] Nega Miherete, The Interface between Access to Genetic Resources, Benefit Sharing and Intellectual Property Right Laws in Ethiopia: Analysis of their Synergies, (2010), A Thesis for the Partial Fulfillment of LL.M., Addis Ababa University, p 94

form.[51]

In 1997 a Texas-based company (Rice Tec) acquired US Patent No. 5,663,484 on basmati rice lines and grains. The patent, with twenty claims, covers alleged novel methods of breeding, preparing, and cooking basmati rice. Rice Tec's claims are for a specific rice plant (Claims 1-11, 14), for seeds that germinate the patented rice plant (Claim 12), for the grain that is produced by that plant (Claims 13, 15-17), and for the method of selecting plants for breeding and propagating particular grains of rice (Claims 18-20). It should be noted that for centuries basmati rice has been grown and developed in the Greater Punjab region, now split between India and Pakistan. Basmati rice is world-famous for its fragrant aroma, long and slender grain, and distinctive taste. Indeed, the Oxford Dictionary defines "basmati" as a "long grained aromatic kind of Indian rice." In 1997 exports of basmati rice constituted 4 percent of India's export earnings. Basmati refers to a particular class or rice, of which there are over 400 varieties in India and Pakistan. Over one million hectares of rice paddy are cultivated in India with basmati rice per annum and 0.75 million hectares are cultivated in Pakistan. In 1998-99 alone India exported US$425 million worth of basmati rice. In this case, the patent on basmati not only appropriated a globally recognized name but also threatened the livelihood of thousands of Punjabi farmers who exported basmati rice.[52]

In 1997 two professors at Colorado State University were asked to abandon patents on Quinoa Chenopodium Quinao, an important food crop among the Andeans. The professors, Duane Johnson and Sarah Ward, applied for and obtained US Patent No. 5,304,718 on a traditional Bolivian variety of quinoa called "Apelawa." This gave them an exclusive monopoly over male sterile plants of this variety and their use in creating other hybrid quinoa varieties. The patent covers both male sterile Apelawa Quinoa and "any" quinoa hybrid that is derived from it. The point here is that male sterility in Andean farmers' varieties of Quinoa had been known for decades among the Andean farmers and peasant farmers in

---

[51] Mgbeoji, Cited above at note 7, p 14

[52] Id, p 15

Bolivia, Peru, Ecuador, and Chile.[53]

Neem, or *Azadirachta indica*, has been used for diverse purposes over centuries in India. It has been used in medicine and agriculture. The *neem* is mentioned in Indian texts written over 2000 years ago as an air purifier and as a cure for almost all types of human and animal diseases because of its insect and pest repellant properties. It is used on every farm, in every house, almost every day in India. Therefore, *neem* is known as the 'free tree' of India. In 1971, US timber importer Robert Larson observed the tree's usefulness in India and began importing neem seed to his company headquarters in Wisconsin. Over the next decade, he conducted safety and performance tests upon a pesticidal neem extract called Margosan-O and in 1985 received clearance for the product from the US Environmental Protection Agency. Three years later, he sold the patent for the product to the multinational chemical corporation, W.R. Grace. Since, 1985, over a dozen US patents have been taken out by US and Japanese firms on formulae for stable *neem* based solutions and emulsions and even for a *neem* based toothpaste. The neem is thus no longer a 'free tree' and has more than ninety patents on it today including patent claims by American, Japanese and German companies. It is now the intellectual property of western scientists and corporations. [54]

2.1.5. Patent as an instrument of stimulating and rewarding

There are different theories concerning the rational for patent; one of which is the Reward Theory. This theory argues that inventions are made because the patent system offers a reward to inventors. According to this argument, without this promised reward there would be no inventions. They further argue that patents serve as incentive for the commercialization and industrialization of inventions. Therefore, the most important role of patent, according to the reward theory, is thus to provide incentive, encouragement, and security to those who want to commercialize inventions.

---

53 Ibid

54 Shiva V., cited above at note 41, pp 57-58

Other groups on the other hand argue that patent never encourage inventions. They argue that the reward theory of patent has some drawbacks; the first is that not all inventions are motivated by expectations of material fortune. And inventions also occur regardless of the existence or non-existence of reward mechanisms. [55]

Another reason the reward theory does not adequately explain the phenomenon of inventiveness is that history is replete with accounts of inventions that were simultaneously created by different inventors in different places. For example, Polzunov in Russia had invented a steam engine before James Watt. Watt got a patent and Polzunov did not. If these inventors had been in the same country, which of them would claim the reward promised by the patent system?[56]

The opponents of the reward theory argue on the contrary that patents are merely used to block others from entry into the market which in other words means protecting an already created monopoly.

Vandana Shiva, a well known Indian scientist, mentions many researchers conducted on this issue. As put by her the researches proved that patents are not the main causes for encouraging invention and economic development. To mention some of them:

A study carried out in 1977 by C.T. Taylor and A. Silberson in United Kingdom of 44 large industrial concerns showed that the impact of patents on the rate and direction of invention and innovation is, on the whole, extremely small in all areas examined, except the non basic chemical industries.[57]

Edwin Mansfield studied U.S. industries on the basis of data from 1981-83. Based on a random sample of 100 firms from 12 industries, patent protection was not essential for electrical equipment, office equipment, motor vehicle, instrument

---

[55] Mgbeoji, Cited above at note 7, p 20

[56] Ibid

[57] Shiva v., cited above at 29, p 13- 13

primary metal, rubber, and textile industry.[58]

Thus, patents are not necessary for developing a climate of invention and creativity. They are more important as instruments of market control.

As already mentioned and the examples reflect; the most "apparently legitimate" factor central to bio-piracy is the patenting of plants and related traditional knowledge. The efforts and knowledge of indigenous people and plants which they have protected, developed and reserved for centuries are being owned and commercialized by giant biotech institutions and the north/industrialized states for the mere fact that they (the indigenous people) didn't passed through the legal process of patenting. So the giants are owning the plants and related traditional knowledge of the indigenous people by using a patent regime. So the later/the south prefer to call this trend a piracy than a legitimate legal mechanism. They mention the patenting system as a means created by the northerners to steal their biological resources and knowledge.[59] Bio-piracy must thus be seen as part of the legal and institutional processes by which powerful states and corporate interest groups seek to control and dominate Third World plant genetic resources and associated knowledge of the uses of plants.

The northerners/industrialized states and big international pharmaceuticals put the aforementioned analysis which is mostly unacceptable in the sight of the least industrialized and biodiversity rich countries (mentioned in some literatures as the south). Therefore, the formers do not put the patenting system as a mechanism stretched to steal the natural resources and related traditional knowledge of indigenous people. They claim that we must look beyond this wide spread and popular assumption that the patent system is merely greedy and monopolistic. The patent system could be said to be both these things and to a certain extent it is true, patents do create monopolies, but to qualify this there are limitations and good reason behind them.

They (industrialized and big pharmaceutical companies) mention the Lockian

---

[58] Id, p 14

[59] Id, p 90

theory of property as one of their ground of argument. As per John Locke's theory of property the world and all in it belongs to everyone; but whenever someone adds some labor to the already existing natural resource then he/she becomes an owner. The fruits of one's labor are one's own because one worked for it hence should be owner for something upon which one added his labor.

The Northerners, hence, argue that this philosophy of "people are entitled to the fruits of their labor, produced by their own intelligence, effort and perseverance" is a philosophy not just created to steal the biodiversity of the southerners rather it is a philosophy which existed long ago and developed through time.

The basic utilitarian justification for the patent system provides that; incentives to 'promote the progress of science' are achieved by this system. Intellectual Property rights protect innovation and creations and reward innovative and creative activity". The patent system is a reward system as society has a "moral obligation to compensate and to reward the inventors". To suggest that the patent system is purely for economic protection and does not provide any incentive to invent would be wrong, as these two things go hand in hand, as Abraham Lincoln stated, "The patent system added the fuel of interest to the fire of genius".[60]

The idea of "bio-piracy" offers the multinationals and the governments that work for them, an easy way to cement forever their regime of monopolies". This simply is not true, monopolies are granted for a small period of time, a period of just twenty years. What the patenting of plant properties actually does is enable small companies to get a foothold in the market.

Instead of a real monopoly taking place, by the largest multinational pharmaceuticals, for which it would be easy to dominate if the patent did not exist, as there would be no opportunity for the smaller companies, the patent system in fact restricts such monopolies. In creating restricted monopolies, which would be disadvantageous to society do not exist.[61]

---

[60] Scutt H., Bio-piracy : A Defense , Intellectual Property Dissertation, (unpublished), p 5
[61] Id, pp 8-9

Therefore, the patent system of a dual importance; first it helps to create a controlled and time limited monopoly while encouraging discoveries by rewarding inventors. This in turn brings a great benefit for a society. [62]

In conclusion the debate lies on the following broad arguments; on the one hand without Intellectual Property rights no one would invest in innovation or creation, unless no other solution is available. Put practically, in society, particularly in the field of pharmaceuticals and drugs there would be very limited development and research taking place, as to do the necessary research and development of drugs costs money. Without patent protection development companies would be at a very real disadvantage competitively, which is not a good practice for a competitive free market economy. On the other hand claims of bio-piracy/misappropriation generally arise where patents and similar exclusive intellectual property rights in genetic resources, which are commonly intended to encourage innovations, are perceived as too broad and are mechanisms created by the developed nations and the big pharmaceuticals to get access to bio-diverse nation's resources, and where such property rights and the commercial exploitation of resources are not accompanied by mechanisms that recognize and remunerate the contributions by previous holders of the utilized resources and associated knowledge they consider it as a theft.

2.2. Bio-prospecting

Bio-prospecting involves the exploration for any biological resource, otherwise termed "biodiversity," or traditional knowledge for potential commercial use. Bio-prospecting is seen a venue of revenue generation from potentially valuable traditional knowledge and genetic resources. In the presence of well-designed laws and contracts, bio-prospecting presents a "win-win" situation where benefits generated can be used for a range of purposes – improvement to livelihoods of indigenous and local communities, biodiversity conservation programs and bio

---

[62] Ibid

technological capacity building.[63] One is not a bio-pirate only because it is bio-prospecting. As has been mentioned earlier; bio-piracy is the appropriation of natural resources and traditional knowledge with potential of commercial exploitation without the prior informed consent of the owning sovereign state / local community and benefit sharing. Bio-prospecting; which some mention as a legalized system of bio-piracy, is a system by which industrialized states and international pharmaceuticals get access to natural resources and traditional knowledge with a prior informed consent of the owning sovereign state and with an agreement of access and benefit sharing. The access and benefit sharing agreement may include some element. The first is access agreement; the country of ownership, of the genetic resource, should first give permission/consent to the entity accessing the resources mostly mentioned as prior informed consent of the state. It may also include conservation deal which is one among the three main objectives of CBD (Convention on Biological Diversity). So anyone who is using the genetic resources of any country, given the prior informed consent of the owning state, should agree and work on the conservation of the resource. The accessed resource may be owned by group of people/community or it might be a traditional knowledge of a community. In such cases the accessing corporation may make an agreement to provide community service. The other element that an access and benefit sharing agreement may include is sharing of related researches that will be done by the corporation. The last one is compensation or benefit sharing. The company getting benefit from the biological resource or traditional knowledge must agree to make payments for the state/community.

There are still different views related with the idea of bio-prospecting. Some still argue that, as also been mentioned above, it is simply the legalized or formal way of monopolization. As provided by Prof. Dr. Hanspeter Mallot there are two approaches in relation to monopolization/patenting of genetic resources. The maximalist approach; this approach is mainly supported by those who believe completely avoiding all kinds of exclusive intellectual property rights related to genetic resources and associated knowledge. They argue that any privatization and

---

[63] Gehl P., Regulating Bio-prospecting: Institutions for drug research, access, and benefit-sharing, (2009)United Nations University Press, USA, p 19

monopolization of genetic resources and related knowledge should totally be avoided because it will at least deprive part of the natural resource or knowledge of a society, even if they access it with prior informed consent or upon benefit sharing, which could have been freely accessed by anyone for the benefit of all. Therefore, as per the proponents of this idea even bio-prospecting is not a fair activity and they equate with bio-piracy.

The second line of argument by others on the opposite side is the minimalist approach. The proponents are in favor of bio-prospecting; and they argue that owners of natural resource/traditional knowledge should participate in the value creation process. That is they contribute their resource and share from the benefits of the commercialization. [64]

The convention (CBD), as will be discussed later, has three main objectives two of which are ensuring access and equitable sharing of benefits. This implies that the convention recognizes bio-prospecting as a legal and fair means of accessing genetic resources. Some mention the convention as a mechanism created by the developed nations and the influence of big international pharmaceuticals to get a legal access to the natural resource and traditional knowledge of biodiversity rich countries of the south.

2.3. International legal instruments

2.3.1. Convention on Biological Diversity (CBD)

The United Nations Conference on Environment and Development (UNCED), which took place in 1992 in Rio de Janeiro, adopted the Convention on Biological Diversity as one of its major documents. It entered into force in December 1993 and as of May 2009, 190 states were Parties to it. It is implemented through regular (by now, biennial) meetings of the Conference of the Parties (COP), which is the governing body of the Convention and decides by consensus. [65]

---

[64] Mallot H., Fair shares or bio-piracy? Developing ethical criteria for the fair and equitable sharing of benefits from crop genetic resources, (2010), Dissertation(unpublished), Munich, p 10

[65] Scutt, cited above at note 60, p 33

In its preamble, the CBD explicitly recognizes sovereign rights of states over their biological resources[66], as opposed to the view that these resources should be regarded as common heritage of mankind and be freely accessible to everyone; hence, domestic access to genetic resources is not regulated by the CBD. The preamble in this regard mentions that 'states have sovereign rights over their own biological resources.' The paragraph explicitly vests the authority to determine access to genetic resources with national governments, subject to national legislation. The preamble also mentions that sovereign ownership over biological resources doesn't necessarily mean that states have right to do whatever they want regarding biological resources. The preamble further provides the responsibility of states; 'states are responsible for conserving their biological diversity and for using their biological resources in a sustainable manner.[67]

The Convention seeks to promote three main objectives conservation of biodiversity, sustainable use of the components of biodiversity, and facilitated access to, and an equitable sharing of the benefits arising out the commercial utilization of genetic resources.

The Convention on Biological Diversity (CBD) has as one of its objectives the fair and equitable sharing of the benefits derived from the utilization of genetic resources, including by appropriate access to genetic resources and by appropriate transfer of relevant technologies, taking into account all rights over those resources and to technologies, and by appropriate funding.

The access and benefit sharing objective of the CBD is the one which directly relates with the issue of bio-piracy or bio-prospecting.

---

[66] Convention on Biological Diversity (hereinafter CBD), Article 3, States have, in accordance with the Charter of the United Nations and the principles of international law, the sovereign right to exploit their own resources pursuant to their own environmental policies, and the responsibility to ensure that activities within their jurisdiction or control do not cause damage to the environment of other States or of areas beyond the limits of national jurisdiction.

[67] See the preamble of CBD

2.3.1.1. Access and benefit sharing

Since 1993, many countries and several regions have established provisions on access and benefit-sharing (ABS) for biological and genetic resources through laws or administrative measures. A wide range of mechanisms have been chosen to regulate access to biological and genetic resources and benefit sharing at the national level. The Parties recognized the significance of experience with ABS systems in the terms of reference they set for the negotiation of the Nagoya Protocol, which drew on an analysis of existing legal and other instruments at national, regional and international levels relating to ABS, including access contracts, experiences with their implementation, and compliance and enforcement mechanisms. The Convention establishes as one of its objectives the fair and equitable sharing of benefits derived from the access to and use of biodiversity. [68]

ABS has been one of the most controversial regulatory and policy issue both nationally and internationally the coming into force of the CBD.

Several countries tried to established provisions on ABS for biological and genetic resources in their laws or administrative structures. However, the fact remains that few countries have chosen a wide range of mechanisms to regulate access to biological and genetic resources and benefit sharing at the national level. Some countries have developed new stand-alone laws on ABS and others have amended, revised or updated existing general biodiversity related laws to introduce and give effect to ABS components. Yet others have promulgated administrative guidelines as they are still in the process of considering legislative options. [69]

As it is reflected from the article below and other provisions of the CBD; the key components of the access and benefit sharing regime of the CBD are (i) sovereignty of the state over genetic resources of its own, (ii) prior informed consent (PIC) from party providing access to biological resource, (iii) mutually

---

[68] Cabrera J. et al., Overview of National and Regional Measures on Access to Genetic Resources and Benefit Sharing: Challenges and Opportunities in Implementing the Nagoya Protocol, (2nd de., 2012), pp 5-6

[69] Ibid,

45

agreed terms (MATs) for access and use of biological resources, and (iv) benefit sharing from access to and use of genetic resources and associated traditional knowledge.[70]

Article 15 of the CBD deals with the issues of access and benefit sharing reads as follows;

1. Recognizing the sovereign rights of States over their natural resources, the authority to determine access to genetic resources rests with the national governments and is subject to national legislation.

2. Each Contracting Party shall endeavor to create conditions to facilitate access to genetic resources for environmentally sound uses by other Contracting Parties and not to impose restrictions that run counter to the objectives of this Convention.

3. For the purpose of this Convention, the genetic resources being provided by a Contracting Party, as referred to in this Article and Articles 16 and 19, are only those that are provided by Contracting Parties that are countries of origin of such resources or by the Parties that have acquired the genetic resources in accordance with this Convention.

4. Access, where granted, shall be on mutually agreed terms and subject to the provisions of this Article.

5. Access to genetic resources shall be subject to prior informed consent of the Contracting Party providing such resources, unless otherwise determined by that Party.

6. Each Contracting Party shall endeavor to develop and carry out scientific research based on genetic resources provided by other Contracting Parties with

---

[70] Parasad K. et al, Access and Benefit Sharing from Genetic Resources, Available at http//: www.icimod.org/abs , Accessed on [11/14/2012]

the full participation of, and where possible in, such Contracting Parties.

7. Each Contracting Party shall take legislative, administrative or policy measures, as appropriate, and in accordance with Articles 16 and 19 and, where necessary, through the financial mechanism established by Articles 20 and 21 with the aim of sharing in a fair and equitable way the results of research and development and the benefits arising from the commercial and other utilization of genetic resources with the Contracting Party providing such resources. Such sharing shall be upon mutually agreed terms.[71]

The idea reflected under article 3 of the CBD is reaffirmed in article 15. According to Ranee Panjabi "one of the most important achievements of this Convention lays in its clear endorsement of the fact that biodiversity is a national resource and not part of the common heritage of mankind.[72] The concept of common heritage of mankind imposes a global juridical right over plant life forms irrespective of the reach of national boundaries and state sovereignty.

The CBD regime on plant life forms involves creating national strategies and plans, policies, and programs on access to plant life based on terms mutually accepted by "supplier" states and "user" entities. The joint reading of sub articles (3) & (7) gives us that the authority to determine access to genetic resources rests with the national governments and is subject to national legislation and each Contracting Party shall take legislative, administrative or policy measures, as appropriate with the aim of sharing in a fair and equitable way the results of research and development and the benefits arising from the commercial and other utilization of genetic resources.

In the process of access and benefit sharing the convention provides that access to valuable biological resources be carried out on "mutually agreed terms" (MAT)

---

[71] CBD, Art. 15

[72] Walter Reid adds: From the standpoint of global biodiversity conservation, the most important thing is that it confirms under international law that biodiversity is a sovereign national resource and that governments have the authority to determine the conditions under which access to that resource is granted. The distinction ... could not be sharper or its implications for conservation more profound.

and subject to the "prior informed consent" PIC of the country of origin.

Thought the convention doesn't clearly provides the definition for the terms MAT and PIC it is meant to strengthen or reaffirm the idea of sovereign ownership of states over their genetic resources.

Regarding PIC article 15 (5) clearly provides that any country or entity who wants to access a genetic resource from any other member country should first get informed approval of the provider state. [73]

There is again the requirement of MAT (Mutually Agreed Terms) as provided under sub article 4 of the same; 'Access, where granted, shall be on mutually agreed terms and subject to the provisions of this Article.' When a microorganism, plant, or animal is used for a commercial application, the country from which it came has the right to benefit. Such benefits can include cash, samples of what is collected, the participation or training of national researchers, the transfer of biotechnology equipment and know-how, and shares of any profits from the use of the resources.[74] The Convention, therefore, implies that the specific bargain between access to the resources and the sharing of benefits will be open for negotiation between the individual user and provider. For this reason, the Convention is said to favor the negotiation of bilateral ABS contracts between resource provider and resource user. Moreover, the authority for determining access to genetic resources is vested in the state and subject to national legislation.

2.3.1.2. Traditional knowledge

Another key provision in the CBD is Article 8(j), which obliges the Parties to the Convention, subject to their national legislation, to:

... respect, preserve and maintain knowledge, innovations and practices of indigenous and local communities embodying traditional lifestyles relevant for the

---

[73] CBD, article 15 (5) 'Access to genetic resources shall be subject to prior informed consent of the Contracting Party providing such resources, unless otherwise determined by that Party.'
[74] Sustaining life on Earth: How the Convention on Biological Diversity promotes nature and human well-being, Secretariat of the Convention on Biological Diversity, 2000

conservation and sustainable use of biological diversity, promote their wider application with the approval and involvement of the holders of such knowledge, innovations and practices, and encourage the equitable sharing of the benefits arising from the utilization of such knowledge, innovations and practices.[75]

Parties are required to respect, preserve and maintain TK with the approval and involvement of the knowledge holders, which are the indigenous peoples and/or local communities themselves.[76]

The cumulative reading of articles 11, 16 (5) and 15 (7) oblige contracting parties to "as far as possible and as appropriate, adopt economically and socially sound measures that act as incentives for the conservation and sustainable use of components of biological diversity." However, the CBD does not take a categorical stand as to whether or not the patent concept is helpful to the ideals of conservation and equitable use of plants and TKUP. It is arguable that the patent system may be one of those economic "measures or incentive" that may play a role in the process of conservation and sustain-able use of plants and TKUP. Further meetings of the CBD Council of Parties (COP) have set forth additional guidelines as to the implementation of the objectives of the CBD.

To further implement the access and benefit sharing objective of the CBD there are further developments, negotiations, protocols, with the aim of developing an international regime on ABS after the coming into force of the convention in 1993.

In May 1998 the COP established a Panel of Experts on ABS for developing basic concepts and exploring options for ABS on mutually agreed terms.

In October 2001, after some meetings in 1999 and 2000, drafted guidelines on ABS in order to assist members and stakeholders with implementation of the CBD.

In April 2002, the COP, on its 6th meeting, adopted the **Bonn Guideline**.

---

[75] CBD, Article 8 (j)
[76] Tansey G. and Rajotte T. (ed.), The Future Control of Food: A Guide to International Negotiations and Rules on Intellectual Property, Biodiversity and Food Security (2008), Earthscan publishing , UK, p 92

2.3.2. The Bonn Guideline (BGL)

The Bonn Guidelines provide a framework for the implementation of the access and benefit sharing components of the CBD. The Guidelines are meant to assist Parties to the CBD when developing and drafting legislative, administrative and policy measures on access and benefit sharing, and also when developing contracts and other arrangements under mutually agreed terms for access and benefit sharing. They assist parties in their efforts to establish administrative legislative or policy measures on access and benefit sharing.

The Guidelines tries to provide the detailed and specific implementation of some provisions of the CBD (Articles 8(j), 10c, 15, 16 & 19) related to access to genetic resources and benefit-sharing. Let us have a look at some the core provisions of the Bon Guideline which are relevant and related with access and benefit sharing.

A) Overall strategies

Article 22 of the guideline provides the line of strategy that should be followed in the process of ABS of GRs. The guideline (Art.22) mentions that Access and benefit-sharing systems should be based on an overall access and benefit-sharing strategy at the country or regional level. This access and benefit-sharing strategy should aim at the conservation and sustainable use of biological diversity, and may be part of a national biodiversity strategy and action plan and promote the equitable sharing of benefits.

B) Prior Informed Consent (PIC) (Articles 24-40)

Prior informed consent is provided under Art. 15(5) of the CBD and provisions of the BGL 24-40 deals with the implementation of the PIC stipulated under the CBD. PIC, as mentioned earlier, is that the competent national authority of the providing country must be informed of the planned research as part of the application process. Therefore one of the prerequisites for access to genetic resources is communicating the competent agency of the host state and getting the permission/consent of it for accessing the concerned genetic resource.

The BGL provides two basic elements, worthy of mentioning, in the process of PIC; basic principles of PIC and elements of PIC.

i) Article 26: Basic principles of PIC system should include

The basic principles of a prior informed consent system should include:

(a) Legal certainty and clarity;

(b) Access to genetic resources should be facilitated at minimum cost;

(c) Restrictions on access to genetic resources should be transparent, based on legal grounds, and not run counter to the objectives of the Convention;

(d) Consent of the relevant competent national authority (ies) in the provider country. The consent of relevant stakeholders, such as indigenous and local communities, as appropriate to the circumstances and subject to domestic law, should also be obtained.[77]

ii) Article 27: Elements of the PIC system may include:

(a) Competent authority (ies) granting or providing for evidence of prior informed consent;

(b) Timing and deadlines;

(c) Specification of use;

(d) Procedures for obtaining prior informed consent;

---

[77] The Bonn Guideline, Art. 26

(e) Mechanism for consultation of relevant stakeholders;

(f) Process.[78]

The Guideline tries further to define some terms in its subsequent provisions. For instance competent authority is a body of Government or national authority governing *ex situ* and *in situ* collection of genetic resources. [79]

Specification of use is also defined in the Guideline. It states that; Prior informed Consent should be based on the specific uses for which consent has been granted. While prior informed consent may be granted initially for specific use(s), any change of use including transfer to third parties may require a new application for prior informed consent. Permitted uses should be clearly stipulated and further prior informed consent for changes or unforeseen uses should be required.[80]

C) Mutually Agreed Terms/MAT (Articles 41-44)

As it is specified under Art 15 (4) of the CBD ABS should be based on the mutually agreed terms between the host/providing state and the accessing company. The BGL further provides the detailed application that states may follow at the time of concluding MAT from articles 41-44.

The following principles or basic requirements could be considered for the development of mutually agreed terms:

(a) Legal certainty and clarity;

(b) Minimization of transaction costs, by, for example

(c) Inclusion of provisions on user and provider obligations;

---

[78] Ibid, Art. 27
[79] Ibid, Art. 32

[80] Ibid, Art. 34

(d) Development of different contractual arrangements for different resources and for different uses and development of model agreements;

(e) Different uses may include, inter alia, taxonomy, collection, research, and commercialization;

(f) Mutually agreed terms should be negotiated efficiently and within a reasonable period of time;

(g) Mutually agreed terms should be set out in a written agreement.[81]

The following elements could be considered as guiding parameters in contractual agreements. These elements could also be considered as basic requirements for mutually agreed terms: (a) Regulating the use of resources in order to take into account ethical concerns of the particular Parties and stakeholders, in particular indigenous and local communities concerned; (b) Making provision to ensure the continued customary use of genetic resources and related knowledge; (c) Provision for the use of intellectual property rights include joint research, obligation to implement rights on inventions obtained and to provide licenses by common consent; (d) The possibility of joint ownership of intellectual property rights according to the degree of contribution.[82]

D) Benefit Sharing (Articles 45-50)

It is one of the basic objective of the CBD, fair and equitable sharing of benefit arising from the utilization of the genetic resource in concern. The benefits might be monetary or non-monetary i.e. samples of what is collected, the participation or training of national researchers, the transfer of biotechnology equipment and know-how, and shares of any profits from the use of the resources. [83] The

---

[81] Ibid, Art. 42

[82] Ibid, Art. 43

[83] Parasad, cited above at note 70

Guideline also provides, under Appendix II, examples of monetary or non-monetary benefit may include. Near-term, medium-term and long-term benefits should be considered, including up-front payments, milestone payments and royalties. The time-frame of benefit-sharing should be definitely stipulated. Furthermore, the balance among near-term, medium-term and long-term benefit should be considered on a case-by-case basis. Pursuant to mutually agreed terms established following prior informed consent, benefits should be shared fairly and equitably with all those who have been identified as having contributed to the resource management, scientific and/or commercial process. The latter may include governmental, non-governmental or academic institutions and indigenous and local communities. Benefits should be directed in such a way as to promote conservation and sustainable use of biological diversity.[84]

The guideline, as mentioned earlier, in intended to create a guideline/framework that each member country should follow in ABS agreements and a framework for national legislations and policies that should be followed by each member states during the negotiation with other states or company. Therefore, the above mentioned, provisions of the BGL tries to list the elements that should/may be included in national legislations and in specific agreements. It should also be noted that the Guideline is not binding, so it up to the states to follow Guideline or to reject it.

To further implement the third objective of the CBD, fair and equitable sharing of benefits, the Nagoya Protocol on Access to Genetic Resources and the Fair and Equitable Sharing of Benefits Arising from their Utilization to the Convention on Biological Diversity (Nagoya Protocol) was adopted at the tenth meeting of the Conference of the Parties to the CBD (COP 10) held in Nagoya, Japan from 18-29 October 2010. A brief discussion on the protocol will be made later on in this paper. Now let us see the TRIPS agreement and its relation with the CBD and related patent issues.

---

[84] The Bonn Guideline, Articles 47-48

2.3.3.   The TRIPs and CBD; Interface
2.3.3.1.   TRIPs and Article 27.3 (b)

The Agreement on Trade-Related Aspects of Intellectual Property Rights (TRIPS Agreement) is one of the more controversial international intellectual property agreements that have entered into force. Its negotiations were highly contentious, and the perspectives of developed and less developed countries on the role of intellectual property protection and enforcement remain far apart.

In 1995, the World Trade Organization (WTO) developed an agreement outlining Trade-Related aspects of Intellectual Property Rights, known as the TRIPS Agreement, which is a comprehensive multilateral agreement concerning intellectual property. As laid out in its preamble, the TRIPS Agreement aims at attempting "to reduce distortions and impediments to international trade, and taking into account the need to pro-mote effective and adequate protection of intellectual property rights, and to ensure that measures and procedures to enforce intellectual property rights do not themselves become barriers to legitimate trade."

Countries that sign the TRIPS Agreement agree to grant patents for any invention, both for products and processes, in all technology fields without discrimination, subject to standard requirements, including the requirements that the invention be novel and industrially applicable. There are, however, three listed exceptions to the TRIPS Agreement general rule regarding patentability. The first exception applies to inventions that violate notions of public morality; specifically excluded are inventions dangerous to the life or health of humans, animals, plants, and the environment. The second exception is that diagnostic, therapeutic, and surgical methods for human or animal treatments may be excluded from being considered patentable per Article 27.3(a). The final exception is especially relevant because it allows TRIPS member countries to effectively eliminate patents for certain substances by allowing countries to exclude from patentability "plants and animals other than microorganisms and essentially biological processes for the production of plants or animals other than non-biological and microbiological processes."

This ability, however, is limited by the TRIPS requirement that any country excluding patentability of plants must provide an effective sui generis system meaning a system of its own as a means of protection.

A brief legislative history of patentability under TRIPS

The patentability of inventions in all fields of technology, a key feature of TRIPS, was one of the issues whose negotiation remained pending until the final phases of the Uruguay Round. Article 27 of the TRIPS Agreement deals with patentable subject matters. Its first paragraph – based on the WIPO Draft Treaty Supplementing the Paris Convention as far as Patents are Concerned establishes the main criteria for patentability: inventions, whether products or process, in all fields of technology, and subject to fulfilling the classical three requirements for patentability: novelty, inventive step and industrial applicability. Paragraphs 2 and 3 of Article 27 contain exclusions to patentability. Paragraph 2 refers to general exclusions which at the time the TRIPS Agreement was negotiated were included in various domestic legislation, but subject to certain conditions. Paragraph 3, however, includes two more specific exceptions to patentability in sub-paragraphs (a) and (b) which need no justification to be applied.[85]

The idea of having worldwide-accepted provisions about patentable subject matter, conditions for patentability and exclusions incorporated in an international treaty was not new in IP negotiations. These components of IP reform were important elements of the negotiations of the WIPO Draft Treaty Supplementing the Paris Convention as far as Patents are concerned. During the WIPO negotiation process and The Hague Diplomatic Conference, the patentability was a heated issue. Two different options about the field of technology were presented to the Diplomatic Conference. One (Option A), was presented by a group of 23 developing countries. This option included many of the elements contained in the current Article 27 of the TRIPS Agreement (inventions contrary to public order, law or morality or injurious to public health; plant or animal varieties or essentially biological processes and methods for medical treatment). Option B referred to the

---

[85] Tansey, cited above at note 76, p 56

patentability of inventions in all fields of technology, without indication of any criteria of patentability or exclusions from patentability. [86]

During the TRIPS negotiations, the first consolidated text of a trade-related IPR agreement was prepared by the chairman and presented in his report to the Negotiating Group in July 1990. This text (the composite text) was mainly based on different proposals previously presented by the European Communities, the US, Japan, Switzerland and a group of 11 developing countries. All these proposals contained a provision about patentable subject matter, though they differed in scope. For instance, all of them, except the one presented by the US, contained exclusions. Among those proposals that incorporated exclusions, the emphasis was quite different. The exclusion of inventions contrary to the public order or morality was included in the proposals presented by the EC, the group of developing countries, Switzerland and Japan; the plant or animal varieties exclusion was included in the proposals of the EC and the group of developing countries, but not in the others. The reference to a sui generis protection system for plant varieties was included for the first time in the proposals made by the EC and Switzerland and was kept in the chairman's consolidated text of July 1990 and in the subsequent texts (the Brussels text of December 1990, the Dunkel text of December 1991 and the final version of the Agreement). [87]

The final drafting of Article 27 contains a built-in review mechanism that was included at the very end of the negotiations in the Brussels text of December 1990, without a time-frame. The four-year term was added to the Brussels text a year later. This built-in review process started in 1999 in the TRIPS Council and has not yet been finalized. [88]

Article 27 of the TRIPs agreement is probably the most controversial, radical and stringent international legal instrument providing minimum standards of patent laws across the globe. It requires the availability of product and process patents for all new and useful products in all fields of technology, without discrimination as to

---

[86] Ibid

[87] Ibid.
[88] Ibid.

subject matter. Article 27 (1) of the TRIPs agreement provides as follows: [89]

Subject to the provisions of paragraphs 2 and 3, patents shall be available for any inventions, whether products or processes, in all fields of technology, provided that they are new, involve an inventive step and are capable of industrial application. [Emphasis added]

The exceptions stated in paragraphs 2 and 3 are:

2. Members may exclude from patentability inventions, the he commercial exploitation of which is necessary to protect prevention within their territory of *ordre public* or *morality*, including to protect human, animal or plant life or health or to avoid serious prejudice to the environment, provided that such exclusion is not made merely because the exploitation is prohibited by their law.

3. Members may also exclude from patentability:

A. diagnostic, therapeutic and surgical methods for the treatment of humans or animals;

B. Plants and animals other than micro-organisms, and essentially biological processes for the production of plants or animals other than non-biological and micro-biological processes. However, Members shall provide for the protection of plant varieties either by patents or by an Effective sui generis system or by a combination of thereof.[90]

Article 27.3 (b) requires member states to provide for a patent protection or an equivalent sui generis system or combination of both for inventions, as far as the invention fulfills the ordinary patentability requirements, on genetic resources and developments of new plant varieties. This mechanism of IP protection on the so called biological inventions is claimed by the south states the long hand influence of US, other developed nations and big international pharmaceuticals to get

---

[89] Mgbeoji, Cited above at note 7, p 44

[90] TRIPs Agreement Article 27

ownership over genetic resources and traditional knowledge of indigenous people.

2.3.3.2. TRIPs and CBD; Conflict or Coexist?

The TRIPs Agreement reflects an important step in the globalization of intellectual property frameworks. One key element of this globalization has been the development under TRIPs agreement. The greatest pressure and diplomatic effort of United States to crystallize intellectual property as a 'trade related issue' under the shield of the World Trade Organization (WTO) culminated in 1994 in the form of the agreement on Trade Related aspects of Intellectual Property Rights (TRIPs).[91] It was clear that since most US exports relied on some form of intellectual property (potentially reproducible without appropriate permission), a greater protection of these commodities in international markets was essential. It came as no surprise then, that most of the developed world viewed the TRIPs Agreement as an integral part of any new international trade order. Despite the TRIPs being viewed as a Faustian bargain by developing countries, underlying power imbalances ensured that the US position was upheld, with developing countries being given additional time to bring their laws into conformity with TRIPS.[92]

The TRIPs agreement is intended to set global minimum standards for intellectual property. The objectives of TRIPs, as stated in Article 7, are to provide for the protection and enforcement of IPRs in a way which promotes technological innovation and the transfer of technology to the mutual advantage of producers and users of technological knowledge.

The relationship between the TRIPS Agreement and the Convention on Biological Diversity (hereinafter "CBD") has become a major focus of discussion in the TRIPs Council within the context of the review of Article 27.3(b). It has been argued, at one end, that the agreements are incompatible and that the TRIPs

---

[91] Vaish V. et al, "Is there a Need to 'Substantially Modify' the Terms of the TRIPS Agreement?", Journal of Intellectual Property Rights, (2012), Vol. 17, Hyderabad India, p 195

[92] Ibid

Agreement should be amended so as to bring it in line with the CBD, while at the other end, it has been claimed that there is no inconsistency.[93]

It is obvious that the two international documents are different from different perspectives. Some of the differences include; difference in objective (CBD; the conservation of biological diversity; the sustainable use of its components; and the fair and equitable sharing of the benefits arising out of the utilization of genetic resources while TRIPs is setting minimum standards), in subject matter they address (CBD; protection of and control over biological diversity and TRIPs setting standards of intellectual property law) and in implementation.[94]

As it is mentioned above, the two instruments regulate different subject matters. However, when we look at the implementation of objectives of the CBD and issues of patentability of inventions over genetic resources regulated under Art. 27 of the TRIPs; there is a clear inconsistency. The CBD is the first international instrument to recognize the sovereign right of states over their biological resources and one of its main objectives promotes access to genetic resources to be made on the basis of prior informed consent of the provider states and a mutually agreed terms as to benefit sharing arising from the commercial utilization of the biological resource the proper implementation thereof. One of the purposes of these requirements under the CBD is to tackle misappropriation of biological resources and acts of bio-piracy.

TRIPS has been criticized for failing to promote the CBD goals of benefit-sharing and informed consent because such issues are not included as requirements to patent protection. The global south/mega diverse developing states are claiming that unless part of the TRIPs regulating patent is revised it merely a provision facilitating bio-piracy or claim it to be a mechanism designed by the developed to access our biological resources and related traditional knowledge.

---

[92] [93] Review of the Provisions of Article 27.3(b) of the TRIPS Agreement Communication by the European Communities and their Member States on the Relationship Between the Convention on Biological Diversity and the
TRIPS Agreement (submitted to the TRIPs Council on 3 April 2001)

[94] Ibid.

The clear inconsistency between CBD and TRIPs lies hear; the CBD, as also mentioned earlier, acknowledges the sovereign ownership of states over their biological resources and the need to equitable sharing of benefits and any access to biological resources to be made after the prior informed consent (PIC) and mutually agreed terms (MAT) with the country of origin.

However, when we come to TRIPs it does not recognize the exercise of national sovereignty of states over their biodiversity. Furthermore, there is no any requirement of benefit sharing, prior informed consent of the origin country or mutually agreed terms before accessing the genetic resource of a state or related traditional knowledge of a community. TRIPs does not require patentees to disclose the country of origin or does not put an obligation on the patentees to fulfill access obligations towards genetic resources. In short terms unless otherwise TRIPs is revised in a way that promotes the principles provided under the CBD, it leaves a wide opened road for bio-piracy.

Therefore, one of the international debate is a bid to reconcile the inconsistencies and to secure the plunder of their genetic resources and traditional knowledge without proper PIC and MAT by user; that developing countries wish for the amendment of the TRIPS agreement to require patent applications for inventions making use of biological resources and traditional knowledge to disclose the origin of the resources or knowledge, (disclosure proposal) and to provide evidence that they have been given informed consent and have complied with national legislation regarding benefit sharing.[95]

2.3.3.3. The Disclosure Requirement

Biological resources are a key resource for many inventions, particularly in the field of medicines. Bio-prospectors mine these resources worldwide based on the knowledge of their benefits available in the public domain, conduct research on them and invent medicines, plant varieties and other biotechnological products and

---

[95] Ibid

patent them with a view to exploit them commercially. More often than not, they do not disclose in their patent applications the origin of these resources or traditional knowledge used in their research. This has resulted in allegations of bio-piracy against them. CBD requires that access to genetic resources should be on 'mutually agreed terms' subject to 'prior informed consent' of the resource provider (Article 15.4/5). The competent authority in the country providing genetic resources is expected to grant access permit to the users. However, there is no mechanism to verify whether PIC and MAT requirements have been complied with.[96]

Under the TIPs agreement, currently, there is no any requirement on member states to include in their respective legislations a mechanism of checking whether there is misappropriation of GRs or TK at the time of accessing before granting a patent protection. Where these patents are granted outside the territories of members owning the genetic resources in question, and since IPRs are limited to the territorial jurisdiction where granted, developing countries, championed by such mega diverse countries, seek an international recognition of the problem and its solution.[97]

Therefore, developing states and mega diverse nations are proposing for the amendment of Article 27.3 (b) to include a disclosure requirement of the country of origin which is an amendment currently being discussed, not only under the agenda of reviewing Article 27.3(b) of the TRIPs but also under the heading of 'implementation issues' at the Doha Round.

The disclosure requirement proposes that the TRIPS Agreement should be amended in order to require that an applicant for a patent relating to biological materials or to traditional knowledge shall provide, as a condition to acquiring patent rights:

[96] Jospeh* R., "International Regime on Access and Benefit Sharing: Where Are We Now?", Asian Biotechnology and Development Review, Vol. 12 No. 3, (2010), p 81, Available at: http://ssrn.com/abstract=1754351

[97] The TRIPS-CBD Issue in the WTO: A South Asian Perspective, Available on http://cutsgrc.org/pdf/CUTS GRC Note on TRIPS-CBD Issues, Accessed on [November 16, 2012]

(i) Disclosure of the source and country of origin of the biological resource and of the traditional knowledge used in the invention;

(ii) Evidence of prior informed consent through approval of authorities under the relevant national regimes; and

(iii)   Evidence of fair and equitable benefit sharing under the national regime of the country of origin.

They argue further that it would be more cost-effective to establish an internationally accepted solution to prevent bio-piracy than to divert national resources to expensive judicial processes for revocation of patents that include illegal genetic resources. Developing countries, in particular the least developed countries do not have the resources to follow each patent issued abroad.[98]

Articles 16 (d) (i) & 53 of the BGL on Access to Genetic Resources and Fair and Equitable Sharing of the benefits Arising out of their Utilization also invites Contracting Parties to encourage the disclosure of the country of origin of genetic resources used in an invention in applications for intellectual property rights (IPRs) as a possible contribution to tracking compliance with prior informed consent and the mutually agreed terms on which access to those resources was granted.

A mandatory obligation on the patent applicant as part of the norms of disclosure would have the following advantages:

(a) It would be an additional reason why the patent applicant would be encouraged to comply with the national laws on ABS;

(b) The onus would be on the patent applicant, so member countries cannot raise the objection of higher administrative costs for the patent office;

---

[98] Ibid.

(c) It would enable patent offices to be more vigilant while examining patent applications that deal with a biological resource and associated TK; and

(d) It would serve as a critical tool for biodiversity rich countries in tracking down applications based on bio-resources and related TK, and enable adequate challenges to suspicious patents.[99]

The biotech industry is ferociously against the disclosure proposal. The American Bio Industry Alliance (ABIA) held that "mandatory disclosure of source and origin on genetic resources and/or related traditional knowledge have failed to provide positive incentives for stakeholders to engage in the ABS process". The Biotechnology Industry Organization (BIO) and International Federation of Pharmaceuticals Manufacturers and Associations (IFPMA) in their joint submission to (IGC WIPO) stated that "these requirements would introduce significant uncertainties into the patent system and would thereby undermine the incentives of patents as a catalyst for innovation" [100]

2.3.4. The Nagoya Protocol

In order to implement the third objective of the CBD (ABS); there have been many efforts and negotiations; though very slow. The COP 5 (2000) established the Ad Hoc Open-ended Working Group on ABS with the mandate to develop guidelines on ABS. The result is the Bonn Guidelines, adopted unanimously by some 180 countries.[101]

The Bonn Guidelines are of voluntary nature with an emphasis on the obligation for users to seek PIC of providers and MAT and has been criticized that the Guidelines focus too much on the access side and thus on provider country

---

[99] Joseph*, cited above at note 96, p 82
[100] Id, p 84

[101] Koutouki K., The Nagoya Protocol: Status of Indigenous and Local Communities, Legal Aspects of Sustainable Natural Resources, Legal Working Paper Series, 2011, pp 9-10, Available on http://cisdl.org/public/docs/legal/The%20Nagoya%20Protocol%20%20Status%20of%20Indiginous%20and%20Loc al%20Communities.pdf, Accessed on [November 19/2012]

measures as opposed to user country measures. The need for user-country measures has therefore been stressed in order to ensure compliance with domestic ABS legislation of the provider country and to monitor the utilization of genetic resources and associated TK to enforce benefit-sharing agreements. Different groups of developing countries including the Group of 77 and China as well as the Group of Like-minded Mega-diverse Countries (LMMC) thus pushed for a protocol on ABS.[102]

After prolonged deliberations lasting over six years, the access and benefit sharing Protocol with regard to genetic resources, laying the foundation for the International Regime, was adopted at the tenth meeting of the Conference of the Parties (COP 10) to the CBD held in Nagoya, Japan from 18-29 October 2010.[103]

One general observation is that, even after 18 years since the entry into force of the CBD, a large number of Parties to the Convention continue to face challenges in the adoption and implementation of functional national ABS laws and measures. According to the CBD Secretariat, to date, only 60 countries have some type of laws, measures or instruments to regulate ABS of genetic resources.[104]

2.3.4.1. Objectives of the Protocol

The **"Nagoya Protocol on Access to Genetic Resources and the Fair and Equitable Sharing of Benefits arising from their Utilization"** is an international instrument with the objective of ensuring the fair and equitable sharing of the benefits arising from the utilization of genetic resources, thereby contributing to the conservation and sustainable use of biodiversity. To advance fair and equitable benefit sharing, the Nagoya Protocol also addresses appropriate access to genetic resources and transfer of relevant technologies.[105] Hence, it is a protocol, international regime, meant to further implement the third objective of the CBD

102 Ibid.

103 Joseph* R., cited above at note 96, p 87
104 Cabrera, cited above at note 68 , p 6

105 Nagoya Protocol on Access and Benefit Sharing -Technical Brief, Union for Ethical Bio Trade, Available at www.ethicalbiotrade.org/resources, Accessed on [November 19/2012]

which is fair and equitable sharing of benefits of genetic and biological resource and issue of access resources.

2.3.4.2. An overview of the core provisions of the Nagoya provisions A) The preamble

The Nagoya protocol is composed of 27 preambular paragraphs, 36 articles, and one annex. The preamble first repeats some of the paragraphs of the preamble of CBD and clarifies the importance of ABS for conservation further when stating that, *"economic value of ecosystems and biodiversity and the fair and equitable sharing of this economic value with the custodians of biodiversity are key incentives for the conservation of biological diversity and the sustainable use of its components."*

The preamble also recognizes role of access and benefit-sharing to contribute to the conservation and sustainable use of biological diversity, the linkage between access to genetic resources and the fair and equitable sharing of benefits arising from the utilization of such resources and promoting equity and fairness in negotiation of mutually agreed terms between providers and users of genetic resources. [106]

The last seven points are concerned with TK highlighting amongst others Article 8(j) CBD, the importance of TK for the conservation of biological diversity, the diversity of circumstances in which TK associated with genetic resources is held or owned by ILC and their right to identify the rightful holder of their TK.[107]

B) Access requirements

[106] Preamble of Nagoya Protocol on Access to Genetic Resources and the Fair and Equitable Sharing of Benefits Arising from their Utilization to the Convention on Biological Diversity (hereinafter Nagoya Protocol)

[107] Koutouki, cited above at note 101, p 11

Access provisions under the Protocol reiterate that, under reaffirmation of sovereign rights over natural resources, access to genetic resources for their utilization is subject to prior informed consent of the providing party.[108]

The Protocol is very elaborate on the procedural facilitation of access. For this purpose, provider states shall provide for 'legal certainty, clarity, and transparency' of their domestic ABS legislation, 'fair and non-arbitrary rules and procedures' on access to genetic resources', 'information on how to apply for prior informed consent', clear, cost-effective and timely decision-making, recognition of a permit or its equivalent as evidence of PIC, criteria and procedures for the involvement of indigenous and local communities, and clear rules and procedures for requiring and establishing MAT (Article 6.3 (a-b) & (f)). [109]

Articles 6.3(g) (i) - (iv) deals with MAT; and provide the requirements that MAT must include. Among others, dispute settlement clauses and terms on benefit sharing, including intellectual property rights; subsequent third-party use; changes of intent; and sharing information on implementation of MAT.

Parties on the provider side that must be involved by giving consent and agreeing on mutual terms include the provider state itself[110] and – according to domestic legislation – indigenous and local communities that hold genetic resources[111] and/or associated traditional knowledge.[112]

Responsible for advising on PIC and MAT are national focal points and

---

[108] Nagoya protocol, Article 6.1

[109] E. K. et al, "The Nagoya Protocol on Access to Genetic Resources and Benefit Sharing: What is New and what are the Implications for Provider and User Countries and the Scientific Community?", Law. Environment and Development Journal , vol. 6/3, (2010), p 250, Available at http://www.lead-journal.org/content/10246.pdf

[110] Nagoya Protocol, Article 6.1

[111] Id, Article 6.2

[112] Id, Article 7

competent national authorities.[113] The latter are responsible for granting access too.[114]

C) Benefit Sharing

Concerning benefit sharing, each party is obliged to take legislative, administrative, or policy measures to ensure that benefits arising from the utilization of genetic resources as well as subsequent application and commercialization are shared fairly and equitably with the providing party.[115] Benefits listed under the Protocol include monetary and non-monetary benefits listed o the Annex of the protocol. [116]

D) Utilization of Genetic Resources

Any utilization of genetic resources generating benefits is a ground for benefit sharing. For this reason, the definition of the term is crucial. The CBD, though it defines genetic resource, It does not give a definition for the term utilization. This protocol, however, defines utilization of genetic resources[117] as *'research and development on the genetic and/or biochemical composition of genetic resources, including through the application of biotechnology as defined in Article 2 of the Convention'*. It is of high importance that R&D on the biochemical composition of the genetic resource is covered. This means that, for instance, drugs based on the extraction of chemicals from biological resources are subject to benefit sharing.[118]

Therefore the **scope of application** the protocol shall be to *genetic resources within the scope of Article 15 of the Convention and to the benefits arising from the utilization of such resources. This Protocol shall also apply to traditional*

---

[113] Id, Article 13.1 & 13.2

[114] Id, Article 13.2

[115] Id, Article 5.1 & 5.5
[116] Id, Article 5.4

[117] Id, Article 2 (c)

[118] Chege, cited above at note 109, p 251-251

knowledge associated with genetic resources within the scope of the Convention and to the benefits arising from the utilization of such knowledge.[119]

E) Indigenous/local community and TK

Communities that hold genetic resources and traditional knowledge associated to genetic resources enjoy extensive consideration within various provisions of the Protocol. First, where communities have the domestic right to grant access to genetic resources or hold traditional knowledge, parties should adopt measures ensuring that PIC and involvement for access is obtained from such communities. [120]Second, benefits derived from the utilization of genetic resources or traditional knowledge held by communities must be shared in a fair and equitable way with such communities.[121] Third, parties, with effective participation of communities, shall establish mechanisms to inform users of traditional knowledge about their obligations.[122]

Fourth, in order to increase awareness of genetic resources and traditional knowledge held by communities, parties shall organize meetings of communities, establish a help desk for communities, and involve communities in the implementation of the Protocol.[123]Fifth, in order to enable effective participation of communities in implementation of the Protocol, capacities of communities need to be improved as well. In this regard, the Protocol emphasizes the need to increase capacities of women[124] owing to their vital role in ABS processes, policy making, and implementation of biodiversity conservation.[125]

F) Compliance

---

[119] Nagoya Protocol, Article 3

[120] Id, Articles 6.2, 6.3 (f) & 7

[121] Id, Articles 5.2 & 5.5

[122] Id, Article 12.2

[123] Id, Articles 21 (b)-(c) & (h)

[124] Id, Articles 23.3 & 22.5 (j)

[125] Chege, cited above at note 109, p 252

Each Party shall take measures to provide that genetic resources, utilized within its jurisdiction have been accessed in accordance with PIC and that MAT have been established, "as required by the domestic [ABS] legislation or regulatory requirements of the other Party ". In addition Parties shall take measures to address situations of non-compliance and cooperate in cases of alleged violation of domestic ABS legislation or regulatory requirements.[126]

Each Party shall take measures to provide that genetic resources, utilized within its jurisdiction have been accessed in accordance with PIC and that MAT have been established, "as required by the domestic [ABS] legislation or regulatory requirements of the other Party ". In addition Parties shall take measures to address situations of non-compliance and cooperate in cases of alleged violation of domestic ABS legislation or regulatory requirements.[127]

The most important requirement for Parties is the designation of one or more checkpoints. Checkpoints shall receive or collect information related to PIC, the source and utilization of the genetic resource and the establishment of MAT and submit it to relevant authorities, the provider party, and the ABS Clearing-House Mechanism.[128]

To facilitate monitoring the Protocol introduces internationally recognized certificates of compliance which "shall serve as evidence that the genetic resource which it covers has been accessed in accordance with PIC and that MAT has been established"[129]. Thereby the already mentioned permit is issued in accordance with Article 6.3(e) shall constitute such a certificate.[130]

Possible checkpoints could for example include the patent application process

---

[126] Nagoya protocol, Article 15

[127] Koutouki, cited above at note 101, p 14
[128] Nagoya protocol, Article 17.1 (a)

[129] Id, Article 17.3

[130] Id, Article 17.2

(in response to the already mentioned critical relationship with IP protection), application processes for government funding for biodiversity-based research and development or market approval processes.[131]

One of the drawbacks of the protocol is that there is no specified obligation of user states to ensure benefit sharing. As before, the enforcement of benefit-sharing duties is left to contractual means,[132] with all the difficulties of forum, litigation costs, and prosecution of titles. The fact that the Protocol does not go further in that direction constitutes a major disappointment for the provider side.

Nevertheless Parties shall take measures regarding access to justice and the utilization of mechanisms regarding mutual recognition and enforcement of foreign judgments and arbitral awards (Article 18.3).[133] Finally, it is the obligation of each party to monitor the implementation of the Protocol and report regularly to the COP as it is provided under Article 29 of the protocol.

2.3.4.2.1. Achievements of the protocol

A) On TK and right of indigenous community

One the new achievements of the protocol are the revision of Article 8 (j) of CBD and protection of indigenous communities' right. The Article is not strong and limited in its wordings.

The Article 8(j) reads:

Each contracting Party shall as far as possible and as appropriate, subject to its national legislation, respect, preserve and maintain knowledge, innovations and practices of indigenous and local communities embodying traditional lifestyles relevant for the conservation and sustainable use of biological diversity and

---

131 Koutouki, cited above at note 101, p 15

132 Nagoya protocol, Article 18

133 Chege, cited above at note 109, p 252

promote their wider application with the approval and involvement of the holders of such knowledge, innovations and practices and encourage the equitable sharing of the benefits arising from the utilization of such knowledge, innovations and practices. [134]

It begins with the words *'...shall as far as possible and as appropriate, subject to its national legislation....'*. In negotiations speak, words like this are hard fought 'get out of jail free' passes designed to weaken State obligation and to limit any inroads into national sovereignty.[135]

Moreover, nowhere does Article 8(j) of CBD speak of the mandatory nature of the 'prior informed consent' and 'benefit sharing' when it comes to the utilization of traditional knowledge (knowledge, innovations and practices) of indigenous peoples and local communities.[136]

Article 15, which is the main article the implementation of which the Seventh COP asked the Working Group on ABS to negotiate, makes no mention of any rights of indigenous peoples and local communities over genetic resources. It begins with an unassailable *'Recognizing the sovereign rights of States over their natural resources, the authority to determine access to genetic resources rests with the national governments and is subject to national legislation'*. There are no 'exit clauses' here and compared with Article 8(j) and States wanted to eliminate any doubts and establish irrefutably their absolute rights over their genetic resources.[137]

One of the options provided by African states and later supported by Canada and New Zealand to tackle the weak wordings of Article 8 (j) is eliminating the word *'subject to national laws'* by the term *'in accordance with national laws'*. This would retain the facilitative role of the State in situations where Parties argued

---

[134] CBD, Article 8 (j)

[135] Bavikatte K. et al, "Towards a People's History of the Law: Biocultural Jurisprudence and the Nagoya Protocol on Access and Benefit Sharing", Law, Environment and Development Journal vol. 7/1 (2011), p 41, available at http://www.lead-journal.org/content/11035.pdf

[136] Ibid

[137] Ibid

that communities within their jurisdiction needed State protection against exploitation. The introduction this term also means rights of communities under the CBD are not dependent on the discretion of States. Canada and New Zealand also argued further that the former wording undermined the treaties that they had with their indigenous peoples which were not 'subject to national law' but were akin to agreements between nations. [138]

This line of argument finally ended up getting recognition under Article 7 of the Nagoya Protocol which reads as:

"In accordance with domestic law, each Party shall take measures, as appropriate, with the aim of ensuring that traditional knowledge associated with genetic resources that is held by indigenous and local communities is accessed with the prior and informed consent or approval and involvement of these indigenous and local communities, and that mutually agreed terms have been established." [139]

B) Recognizing customary laws and community protocol

France at a rather late stage in the negotiations had received instructions from their foreign ministry to under no circumstances agree to any references to 'customary laws, community protocols and indigenous and local community laws' that were prevalent in the draft Protocol text. It was supported by other European countries later. France proposed the term 'community level procedures' as an alternative to 'customary laws and community protocols'. This was rejected by the African indigenous people's organizations with the support of the African Group arguing that 'community level procedures' were a euphemism for State control and lacked the authenticity of genuine community processes.[140]

However the final wording in the Nagoya Protocol in Art 12.1 now reads:

In implementing their obligations under this Protocol, Parties shall in

---

[138] Ibid

[136] [139] Nagoya Protocol, article 7
[137]
[140] Bavikatte, cited above at note 135, p 45- 46

accordance with domestic law take into consideration indigenous and local communities' customary laws, community protocols and procedures, as applicable, with respect to traditional knowledge associated with genetic resources. [141]

C) Right over genetic resources

The CBD never made a reference as to rights of communities over their genetic resources. Many of the group members in the negotiation process agreed to recognize right of community over genetic resources, however, they further argued that the recognition must be made only by national laws not under an international regime; though resisted by the Africans. [142]

Finally a compromise text was developed and agreed to by all Parties and is now in the Nagoya Protocol. Article 6.2 reads:

"In accordance with domestic law, each Party shall take measures, as appropriate, with the aim of ensuring that the prior informed consent or approval and involvement of indigenous and local communities is obtained for access to genetic resources where they have the established right to grant access to such resources." [143]

The provision is a mandatory provision as it depicts the obligation of the parties by the word 'shall'. At the end of the provision there is this phrase stating '….where they have established right….' This provision shows the recognition that is given to the ownership right of community over their genetic resources. However, the word is neither defined nor clearly provided thereby leaving it to interpretation as to whether these rights are established in national or international law. [144]

2.3.4.3. Nagoya Protocol and the Disclosure Requirement

---

[141] Nagoya Protocol, Article 12.1

[142] Bavikatte, cited above at note 135

[143] Nagoya Protocol, Article 6.2

[144] Bavikatte, cited above at note 135

Developing countries are particularly interested in the EU and its member states establishing effective measures ensuring that GR have been acquired in accordance with PIC and MAT in compliance with provider countries' national ABS legislation. Such measures by developing user countries are required in order to prevent misappropriation ("bio-piracy"). The formers have long demanded a mandatory disclosure of origin of GR and TK in patent applications as an effective means to ensure applicants lay open where and under what conditions they acquired the resources, and thus to allow to check whether they were acquired legally, in accordance with PIC and MAT.[145]

The NP vaguely regulates the issue of 'disclosure requirement' under Article 17 and other related provisions.

Article 17:

1. To support compliance, each Party shall take measures, as appropriate, to monitor and to enhance transparency about the utilization of genetic resources. Such measures shall include:

(a) The designation of one or more checkpoints, as follows:

(i) Designated checkpoints would collect or receive, as appropriate, relevant information related to prior informed consent, to the source of the genetic resource, to the establishment of mutually agreed terms, and/or to the utilization of genetic resources, as appropriate;

(ii) Each Party shall, as appropriate and depending on the particular characteristics of a designated checkpoint, require users of genetic resources to provide the information specified in the above paragraph at a designated

---

[145] Christiane et al, Intellectual Property Rights on Genetic Resources and The Fight Against Poverty, 2011, , Belgium, European Parliament's Committee on Committee on Development, Available at http://www.europarl.europa.eu/activities/committees/studies.do?language=EN, Accessed on [October, 15/2012], p 47

checkpoint. Each Party shall take appropriate, effective and proportionate measures to address situations of non-compliance;

Checkpoint which the protocol orders to be established by each state collects and receives information related with PIC, MAT and the utilization of genetic resource; moreover parties are required to take appropriate measures of non compliance. Permits issued by user countries can serve as (non-obligatory) internationally recognized certificates of compliance that contain such relevant information. However, the NP doesn't further explain what these checkpoints could include. In this context, it would also make particular sense to consider establishing **'patent offices'** as obligatory checkpoints. The Nagoya Protocol itself leaves the choice of which institutions be designated as checkpoints to individual parties. Under the Nagoya Protocol, parties instead agreed to designate one or more "checkpoints" to collect or receive relevant information so as to monitor the uses of GR/TK. [146] The mandatory disclosure requirement at the state of patenting of inventions from genetic resources which had widely been discussed in the run-up to COP10 was not included in the Protocol. [147]

---

[146] Developing countries had high expectations in Nagoya, Carlos Correa said. One of their aims was to find solutions to the problem of bio-piracy. A group of countries had already proposed to amend the TRIPS Agreement in order to include a disclosure requirement for genetic resources in patent applications, he added. Yet they failed to obtain the inclusion of an equivalent provision in the Protocol. The only alternative left was the so called "check point" option. The Nagoya Protocol requires parties to set up one or more checkpoints for prior informed consent, and to monitor whether they are complying with the protocol. This leaves open the possibility for countries to require disclosure should patent offices be designated as such a check point. Nevertheless, Correa stressed that the checkpoint option is a weak alternative to a proper disclosure requirement, since countries have wide latitude in designating their checkpoints. The Nagoya Protocol does not include a list of mandatory checkpoints, among which many biodiversity-rich developing countries had proposed the inclusion of patent offices. (What Comes After Nagoya? Addressing Developing Country Needs in Intellectual Property Rights and Biodiversity, UNCTAD & ICTSD side event, a report, 2011, Available at http://ictsd.org/downloads/2011/05/ictsd-unctad-what-comes-after-nagoya-report.pdf, Accessed on [November, 22/2012])

[147] Chege, cited at note 109, p 257

Chapter Three

3. The Access and Benefit Sharing (ABS) Regime of Ethiopia

3.1. Introduction

With its dramatic geological history, broad latitudinal spread and immense altitudinal range, Ethiopia spans a remarkable number of the world's broad ecological regions. This variety of habitats also supports a rich variety of different species, which contributes to the overall biological diversity (or "biodiversity") of the country. [148]Ethiopia encompasses an extraordinary number of ecological zones, which in turn host rare and endangered species and high rates of endemism. In combination with its importance as a center of genetic and agricultural diversity, the conservation of Ethiopia's biodiversity is an issue of global importance. With the second-largest population in Africa, limited capacity to manage natural resources, and widespread land degradation, however, Ethiopia also faces many serious challenges to efforts to conserve its biodiversity and forests. Species biodiversity in Ethiopia includes 280 mammals, 861 birds, 201 reptiles, and more than 6,000 plants with high rates of endemism. According to the International Union for the Conservation of Nature's (IUCN's) 2007 "red list" of these species, Ethiopia has 6 that are critically endangered, 23 endangered, and 70 vulnerable. Nine national parks, 4 wildlife sanctuaries, 7 wildlife reserves, and 18 controlled-hunting areas have been established in Ethiopia to protect and conserve its valuable biodiversity assets. Of these, however, only two, Simien National Park and Awash National Park, have been officially gazetted. Protected areas in Ethiopia also have suffered from inadequate security, staffing, and equipment, leading to many cases where their status is little more than nominal and providing no protection for their fauna and flora.[149]

---

148 [148] National Biodiversity Strategy and Action Plan, Government of the Federal Democratic Republic of Ethiopia, Institute of Biodiversity of Conservation, December 2005, Available at http://www.cbd.int/doc/world/et/et-nbsap-01-en.pdf, Accessed on [November 27/2012], p ix
[149] GOVERNMENT OF THE FEDERAL DEMOCRATIC REPUBLIC OF ETHIOPIA, INSTITUTE OF BIODIVERSITY CONSERVATION NATIONAL BIODIVERSITY STRATEGY AND ACTION PLAN, 2005, pp 12-13

Threats to Ethiopia's biodiversity, tropical forests, and resource base can be broadly linked to the following categories: limited governmental, institutional, and legal capacity; population growth; land degradation; weak management of protected areas; and deforestation. These threats are largely interrelated and self-reinforcing, whether they are direct (such as charcoal-driven deforestation) or indirect (such as limited governmental capacity as seen in the lack of enforcement of natural resource related policies). It is therefore important not only to understand the individual threats but also to examine them in a holistic fashion that recognizes their interrelation and to address these threats with a multi sectoral approach.[150]

One may question that though we have all these biodiversity resources; is bio-piracy really a treat to Ethiopia? Generally there is a current threat over those nations having wide range of biodiversity resources as there is race of owning genetic resources either through misappropriation or patent protection gained improperly or to the determent of the owning state or community. Coming to Ethiopia there is a living case of our loss over the genetic resource 'Teff'. The case shows the eminence and how prone we are to bio-piracy.

3.2. The case of 'Teff'; a Breif story and Stutus quo

'Teff' is an interesting grain used for centuries as the principal ingredient of the Ethiopian population diet. The principal meal in which 'Teff' is used is called 'enjera': a big flat bread or pancake, than is eaten alone or with any kind of meats, vegetables and sauces. 'Teff' is the smaller grain ever known, and even that it has been demonstrated that it was used by Egyptian Pharaohs; it is until two decades ago that it became the issue of agronomic, nutritional, food technological, microbiological, chemical and physical research. 'Teff' can be used too in all kind of bakery products, beverages, sauces ingredient and porridges. This grain is used too as a livestock. The potential of this grain as an interesting raw material to new food products development is due principally to its protein composition: it is gluten

---

[150] Ethiopia Biodiversity and Tropical Forests 118/119 Assessment, U.S. Agency for International Development, Bureau for Africa, Office of Sustainable Development (AFR/SD), USAID,2008, pp 1-2

free and it has a very high quality of amino acid composition. It is compared with egg protein and with an ideal protein for children between two and five years old. A lot of scientific people have been demonstrated that 'Teff' starch has a low glycemic acid, and that it has a mineral composition better than this or other cereals. That's why; this microscopic grain is beginning a big war between different grain producers and processors. Some companies want to demonstrate that human been needs to include 'Teff' as an important component of his diet. This is against the economical interests of other big companies and associations, as this that grow harvest, mill, process and storage wheat flour.[151]

'Teff' belongs to the genus Eragrostis, which is one of a large family of wild grasses. It originated in and was domesticated in Ethiopia and is grown as a cereal. 'Teff' is an important cereal at the national level. Ethiopia is the only country that is a source of genetic diversity for 'Teff'. 'Teff' has as much or even more food value than major grains such as wheat, barley and maize (Note 18). Moreover, grains such as wheat, rye, barley, and derivatives of these grains contain gluten. Gluten intolerance (coeliac disease or gluten sensitivity) is 'a lifelong autoimmune disorder in which a person's body cannot tolerate a group of grain proteins known as gluten' (Note 19). Since 'Teff' is gluten free, it can be used for the preparation of foods for gluten-intolerant individuals (Note 20). In Ethiopia, 'Teff' grain is ground into flour and fermented for the preparation of 'Teff' based foods (Note 21). 'Teff' flour is the preferred grain for preparing 'injera', a traditional gluten-free pancake (Note 22). The traditional uses of 'Teff' flour also include the preparation of 'Teff' bread and a pudding (;genfo'), while 'Teff' grain is used to make local alcoholic drinks such as 'tella' and 'katikala'(Note 23).[152]

A brief story of what happened

The 'Teff' Agreement, negotiated in March 2004, finalized in December 2004 and signed in April 2005. The parties to this agreement were the Ethiopian Institute

---

151 Patricia (Dr.), TEFF "Survey on the nutritional and health aspects of Teff (Eragrostis Teff)", 2008, p 120

152 Abeba Tadesse (Corresponding Author), "Material Transfer Agreements on 'Teff' and Vernonia – Ethiopian Plant Genetic Resources", Journal of Politics and Law, Vol.2, No.4, 2009 Denmark

of Biodiversity Conservation (IBC), together with what was then the Ethiopian Agricultural Research Organization (EARO), and the Dutch company Health and Performance Food International (HPFI).

The story of the cooperation between Ethiopia and the Netherlands on 'Teff' genetic resources started in 1997, three years after Ethiopia had According to Dr Arnold Mulder and Dr Lodewijk Turkensteen, this company was officially established on 28 July 2005, but 'set up' in 2004 and initiated already in 2003. As can be seen from the timeline, the patent application to EPO was filed under the name HPFI in July 2004 and the ABS agreement on 'Teff' was finalized in December 2004 and signed in March 2005 with HPFI as the user. Ethiopia ratified the CBD through Proclamation No. 98/1994. Larenstein University of the Netherlands, which had by then been involved in tropical agriculture for almost one hundred years, started collaboration with Mekelle University and Alemaya University of Ethiopia on two 'Teff' projects. These projects were warmly welcomed from the Ethiopian side, since 'Teff' had received scant attention in Ethiopian research and development due to other priorities, but had remained a major staple crop of significant importance for nutrition in the country. It was hoped that joint research could help to boost the development of 'Teff' production for the benefit of Ethiopia.[153]

In 2000, the two Dutch inventors Mr A.L. Buwalda and Dr A.J.O. van Velden, who had a small company called Awenyddion, learned about 'Teff' from Mr Meinders of Larenstein University. Mr Meinders was involved in collaborative 'Teff' projects with institutions in Ethiopia, and Larenstein University ran small experiments with 'Teff' in the Netherlands with the involvement of students. The two inventors embraced the idea of growing 'Teff' in the Netherlands and ran a small field experiment. However, this first trial was not very successful as far as yield was concerned.[154]

---

[153] Andersen R. et al, The Access and Benefit-Sharing Agreement on 'Teff' Genetic Resources Facts and Lessons, ABS Capacity Development Initiative for Africa, FRIDTJOF Nansen Institute, Norway, 2012, p 13.

[154] Id., p 33

In 2002, Hans Turkensteen contacted Debre Zeit Agricultural Research Centre, located southeast of Addis Ababa, concerning access to 'Teff' varieties that could perform well in cold climates. According to Jans Roosjen, the harvest of 'Teff' in the Netherlands was about 1000 kg per hectare in 2002. It was important to improve the yield, and access to suitable Ethiopian varieties was seen as the key.[155]

The request from Hans Turkensteen served as the point of departure for negotiations that led to the Memorandum of Understanding (MoU) on Research and Development of International Markets for 'Teff' -based Products between EARO (Dr Demel Teketay, Director General), Larenstein University (Henk Dijk, Director of Larenstein) and Soil and Crop Improvement Company (S&C) (Hans Turkensteen as Director of S&C).[156]

The objectives of the MoU were listed as being to 'strengthen the position of Ethiopia as a leading 'Teff'producer in commercializing the inter -national market for 'Teff' based gluten-free products, encompassing a wide variety of products suitable for consumers with and without intolerance to gluten', 'support Ethiopia to further develop local and international markets for 'Teff' based products' and 'assist and strengthen 'Teff' research and production in relation to the project in Ethiopia'.

In 2003, Debre Zeit Agricultural Research Centre sold 1,440 kg of teff seeds to Larenstein University for research and development purposes: 120 kg each of 12 specified teff varieties. The sale was made known in a letter 'to whom it may concern' from the manager of Debre Zeit Agri-cultural Research Centre, Dr Solomon Assefa, on 21 August 2003, and in which reference was made to the MoU.[157]

On 22 July 2003, S&C filed a patent on the processing of 'Teff' flour in the Netherlands. In autumn 2003, S&C-produced 'Teff' flour was introduced to the market in the Netherlands for the first time.

---

[155] Id., p 35

[156] Ibid.

[157] Andersen, cited above at note 153 , p 39

In July and August 2003, two different Dutch magazines announced that S&C had patented the production and processing of 'Teff' in the European Union. At that time this was in fact not true, but it indicates that rumors regarding the patent application were already circulating.

Later on the Ethiopian government requested EARO (now EIAR) to bring S&C into negotiations with the IBC (because currently, the mandate to negotiate access and benefit sharing agreement is given to IBC), in order to enter into a formal agreement with the IBC on behalf of Ethiopia and the company agreed.[158]

Due to internal disagreement in S&C, as a result a new company named Health and Performance Food International (HPFI) was established. The directors of HPFI itself were Hans Turkensteen and Jans Roosjen, participating in the company through their private companies Tucko Beheer BV and Roosjen BV respectively. S&C continued to exist, but now treated as a subordinate part of HPFI.[159]

On 22 July 2003, S&C filed a patent application in the Netherlands for the processing of 'Teff' flour. On 22 July, 2004, – HPFI files a patent application on the processing of 'Teff' flour with the EPO. On 10 January, 2007, EPO publishes the granting of the 'Teff' patent (EP 1 646 287 B1).

The 'Teff' Agreement between the IBC and EARO or the 'Agreement on access to, and benefit sharing from, 'Teff' genetic resources', was signed on 5 April 2005. It was signed by Dr Girma Balcha on behalf of the IBC and Mr Hans Turkensteen on behalf of HPFI. The Ambassador of the Kingdom of the Netherlands to Ethiopia, Mr. Rob Vermaas and Dr Tewolde Berhan Gebre Egziabher signed as witnesses.

Besides the agreement, the company has undertaken to share the following monetary and non monetary benefits arising out of the utilization of 'Teff' GRs:

---

[158] Id., p 43

[159] Id., p 48

- To pay 1% of the average gross net income of the years 2007-2009;

- Annually royalty of 30% of t`he net profit from sale of basic and certified seeds of 'Teff' varieties specified in the agreement;

- To contribute 5% of its net profit to the Financial Resource Support for 'Teff' (FiRST) that aimed at improving the living conditions of local farming communities and developing 'Teff' business in Ethiopia. This contribution was agreed not to be less than 20,000 Euro per year;

- To share research results, knowledge or technologies with IBC and EARO, except when those are identified to be undisclosed information;

- To involve Ethiopian scientists in 'Teff' research; and

- To establish profitable 'Teff' businesses in Ethiopia ('Teff' farming, cleaning, milling enterprises, bakeries, etc) so that access to 'Teff' genetic resources can be linked to improvement of local economy and poverty eradication.

- Intellectual property rights are addressed in Article 5: 'the company shall neither claim nor obtain intellectual property rights over the genetic resources of 'Teff' or over any component of the genetic resources' (Art. 5.1 of the agreement).
- Article 6 on transfer to third parties establishes that the company cannot transfer 'Teff' seed or 'any component of the genetic resources of 'Teff' to third parties without the explicit written consent of the IBC and other detailed benefit sharing regimes and penalties were included in the agreement. [160]

Implementation problems and status quo

A big problem of communication started to grow between IBC and HPFI. Then the HPFI applied and was declared bankrupt in 2009. The IBC was not officially informed about the bankruptcy until more than a year after the event. Nor was the

---

[160] Id., p 61

Ethiopian institution aware of any impending bankruptcy, as the HPFI Company had breached central reporting and monitoring provisions.

The two directors of S&C/HPFI/the people behind HPFI had set up a new company called Prograin BV/Ecosem 'at least two years before the bankruptcy and for the same purposes as HPFI/S&C. Prior to the bankruptcy, values were transferred from the old to the new companies. Most importantly, HPFI sold the 'Teff' patent for EUR 60,000 to a partnership composed of the HPFI directors, and seed stocks were taken over from HPFI by the new companies. These companies continued to produce and sell 'Teff' flour and 'Teff' products, and to expand their activities to other countries and continents. Since it was HPFI that had been the party to the agreement, and HPFI was now bankrupt, these new firms, even though operating under the same directors and partly the same owners, could continue selling 'Teff' flour and 'Teff' products without being bound by the obligations of HPFI towards Ethiopia.[161]

The On 1 February, 2011, the deadline for filing a notice of appeal with EPO. It has already expired before we made any appeal. After this he only option left for Ethiopia in light of appeal is only to file on a country by country basis among the EPO member countries.

The letter from the IBC to the public receiver in the Netherlands, sent in November 2011, highlighted severe breaches of the 'Teff' Agreement. Citing the provisions of that agreement, the letter put forward the following claims:

That any company established by the former owners of HPFI, including Ecosem, be prohibited from using 'Teff' genetic resources received through the 'Teff' Agreement.

That the 'Teff' patent be withdrawn, in particular if the patent had been transferred to a third party – Ecosem or to any other company owned by the previous owners of HPFI.

---

[161] Id., p vi

84

That Ethiopia must receive its shares of any license fees received for registered 'Teff' varieties, as defined in Annex 2 of the 'Teff' Agreement for the period from the agreement was signed and until its termination

That the plant variety protection of these varieties be considered terminated.

That monetary benefits be shared according to the agreement: specifically, a lump sum that was expected to accrue based on financial performance in 2007, 2008 and 2009; annual royalties of 30% of the net profits from seed sales; license fees; and 5% of net profits (min. EUR 20,000 per year) to a fund to improve the living conditions of local farming communities and for developing 'Teff' business in Ethiopia.

That a penalty of EUR 50,000 be paid to the IBC for HPFI's breach of specified provisions of the 'Teff' Agreement. That an additional penalty be paid for HPFI's failure to fulfill its financial obligations, to be calculated by the public receiver, according to the relevant provisions of the 'Teff' Agreement.[162]

Currently a joint committee is established to deal with possible remedies and further proceedings concerning our loss over 'Teff'.

As has been mentioned, therefore, as Ethiopia is a biodiversity rich country the treat over our genetic resources of the biological diversity and related traditional knowledge is real and eminent. The aforementioned case and ongoing debates on 'Teff' is a clear indicator of the situation.

The main means, used by many countries, to tackle this internationally declared war on genetic resources and biodiversity is building a prudent legal system. Ethiopia, accordingly, has enacted legislations on access an benefit sharing (Proclamation no. 482/2006 A Proclamation to provide for Access to Genetic Resources and Community Knowledge, and Community Right) and Regulation no. 169/2009 on Access to Genetic Resources and Community Knowledge, and

---

[162] Id., p 124

Community Right. Therefore, it is time for Ethiopia to look at its legal system in light of international instruments and strengthen it in a way that best fights bio-piracy.

These two legislations provide the legal/substantive and institutional regimes of the Ethiopian ABS regime. The way the ABS system in which others get access to Ethiopia is regulated determines how well regulated is our system in fighting up against bio-piracy. Therefore, under this chapter I will provide the brief description of the legal and institutional regime and how well regulated is our system to stand against bio-piracy in this and next chapter.

The Patent Claims

According to the publication papers, the invention in question covers 29 specific claims, including a combination of product and process claims. First of all, it covers a floor of a grain belonging to the genus Eragrostis, preferably Erarostis 'Teff', with what it calls a particularly high falling number (at the moment of milling at least 250, preferably at least 380). This high falling number should be achieved, according to the claims, through after-ripening of the grain for at least 4 weeks or preferably at least 8 weeks after harvesting. A further patent claim is that the grain is milled into flour after this after-ripening period, thereby achieving a higher falling number than at harvesting. Furthermore, the flour is ground to a powder so fine that it can pass through a sieve with maximum pore size of 150 microns. The flour to be covered by the 'Teff' patent is gluten-free and is described as containing minimum values of iron, calcium and mineral-binding substance. The patent claim also defines the composition of carbohydrates in the flour. Furthermore, the patent claims cover a dough or batter made from this flour, as well as a food product with such flour. Also according to the patent claims, the 'Teff' patent covers a method for baking a product, involving three steps: a) preparing a dough or batter by mixing flour with a liquid and, optionally, a leavening agent; b) kneading this dough into the desired shape; and c) heating the dough for some time. Baked products prepared according this method are also covered by the patent, as well as a food product or luxury food product prepared from unground 'Teff' grain with a falling number of at least 250. Finally, the patent claims cover methods for binding a composition, preferably a pharmaceutical or cosmetic composition, of at least two components, involving mixing components with starch from flour produced according to the claims of the patent

3.3. Patentability under the Ethiopian law and the TRIPs

TRIPS agreement is the first globally adopted treaty to include patenting of life forms by requiring member states to provide patent protection to all fields of technology. The TRIPs agreement requires WTO members to make patents available for any inventions whether products of processes, in all fields of technology without discrimination provided that they are new, involve an inventive step and are capable of industrial application. [163]

Paragraphs 2 and 3 of Article 27 provide some exceptions for the above scope patentable subject matters of 27.1. Members may exclude from patentability inventions, the prevention within their territory of the commercial exploitation of which is necessary to protect *ordre public or morality*

(27.2) and diagnostic, therapeutic and surgical methods for the treatment of humans or animals; plants and animals other than micro-organisms, and essentially biological processes for the production of plants or animals other than non-biological and microbiological processes (27.3 (a b)). [164]

The first exclusion of *'ordre public'* or *'morality'* is only available in case when the prevention of the commercial exploitation of the biotechnological invention is necessary to protect the morality of the society. If such inventions are made for non-commercial purpose, for instance for scientific research, patent protection could be granted. And the later exclusion gives liberty for member states to exclude from patentability plants and animals and essentially biological processes for the production of plants or animals. However, members have obligation to extend protection to micro-organisms and non-biological and microbiological

---

[163] The TRIPs agreement, Article 27.1

[164] Id., Article 27.2 & 27.3 (a) &(b)

processes.

Coming to the Ethiopian Proclamation Concerning Inventions, Minor Inventions and Industrial Designs, Proclamation NO.123/1995 is the relevant legislation dealing with innovations and patentability. As per this proclamation invention is defined as *"an idea of an inventor which permits in practice the solution to a specific problem in the field of technology."* [165]

The definition of 'invention' under the proclamation does not specifically exclude naturally existing things. Even though discoveries are excluded under Article 4(1) (a) of the proclamation, for the purpose of a better clarity, it is nice to limit further what constitutes a patentable invention. A number of developing countries have a provision which excludes naturally existing things and discoveries from the ambit of invention. [166]

When we come to our legal system Article 4 (1) (a) of the proclamation (123/1995) provides that inventions that are contrary to public order or morality are excluded from patentability. The main difference between this provision and that of the TRIPs is; unlike the TRIPs our legal system excludes from patentability any inventions contrary to ordre public or morality even if made for non-commercial purpose i.e. not compatible with TRIPs in this regard.

Patenting of life forms may be excluded based on Article 27.2 of the TRIPS agreement on the ground of protection of morality. However, the exclusion is only available in case when the prevention of the commercial exploitation of the biotechnological invention is necessary to protect the morality of the society.[167] Under our law biotechnology inventions may be excluded only for reason of morality; which shows a clear inconsistency with the TRIPs. Therefore, contrary to the TRIPs, patenting of life forms is immoral in our society's context which is also

---

[165] Proclamation 123/1995, Article, 2 (3)

[166] Israel Bagashaw, 2010, The Ethiopian Patent Regime and Assessment of its compatibility with TRIPS Agreement, Unpublished, Addis Ababa University, pp 36-37

[167] Proclamation 123/1995, Article 4 (1) (a)

reflected under our legislation.

According to Article 4(1) (b) of the proclamation, plant and animal varieties and essential biological processes for the production of plants or animals are excluded from the subject matter of patentability. Plant variety is defined under the plant breeders right proclamation *"variety means a plant grouping within a single botanical taxon of the lowest known rank which can be: defined by the expression of the characteristics resulting from a given genotype or a combination of genotypes; distinguished from any other plant grouping by the expression of at least one of the said characteristics and considered as a unit for being propagated unchanged."[168]* However, we do not find a clear stipulation as to the exclusion or inclusion of micro-organisms, non-biological and microbiological processes under the Ethiopian patent regime.[169]

Article 27.3 (b) of the TRIPs obliges member states to provide for the protection of plant varieties either by patents or by an effective *sui generis* system or by any combination thereof. This protection for new plant varieties has a negative impact especially for least developed countries like Ethiopia whose economy is largely dependent on small scale farming and conservation and development of seeds is largely in the hands of individual farmers. Hence, our law also excludes the patentability of plant varieties under Article 4(1) (b) of the patent proclamation 123/95.

Since the main objective of this paper is not dealing with the compatibility of our legal regime with TRIPs; it is enough to compare only the relevant provisions (related with patentability of life forms) of the TRIPs and our legal system.

3.4. Access and Benefit Sharing Regime of Ethiopia

The issue of access and benefit sharing came into the attentions of scholars and

---

[168] Proclamation to Provide for Access to Genetic Resources and Community Knowledge and Community Rights, Proclamation No.482/2006, Fed. Neg Gaz, year 13th ,No. 13, Article 8 (hereinafter the ABS Proclamation)

[169] Israel Begashaw, cited above at note 166, p 50

the legislator after the adoption of the CBD in 1994. And hence, though very late and after many improper access and utilization of our resources, a legal regime on access and benefit sharing arising from the utilization of genetic resources has been enacted in the year 2006. Proclamation No. **482/2006; A Proclamation to provide for Access to Genetic Resources and Community Knowledge and Community Right** and to implement the proclamation a subsequent regulation, **Regulation no. 169/2009 on Access to Genetic Resources and Community Knowledge, and Community Right** were issued. From these two pertinent legal let us see the legal and institutional skeleton of our legal regime on the issue at hand and the implication thereof on bio-piracy.

3.4.1. Proclamation No. 482/2006; A Proclamation to provide for Access to Genetic Resources and Community Knowledge, and Community Right

3.4.1.1. The Preamble

Ethiopia is member to the CBD; and one of the main objectives of the convention is conservation and sustainable utilization of genetic resources. The preamble also forwards the importance of conservation and sustainable utilization of the immense biodiversity wealth of Ethiopia for the development of its people;[170] reminding also that Ethiopia is part to the CBD.[171]

Community Right

The preamble also recognizes Ethiopian communities' contribution and their right of ownership. It reads: *'whereas, it is necessary to recognize the historical contribution Ethiopian communities made to the conservation, development and sustainable utilization of biodiversity resources;'[172]*

It further mentions the importance of the proclamation in protecting the

---

[170] See the first paragraph of the Preamble

[171] See the first paragraph of the Preamble

[172] See the first paragraph of the Preamble

knowledge of Ethiopian communities generated and accumulated with respect to the conservation and utilization of genetic resources and promote the wider application of such knowledge with the approval and sharing benefits by such communities; and the importance of the involvement of communities in the making of decisions concerning the use of genetic resources and community knowledge and sharing of benefits derived from the utilization thereof; [173]

Therefore, we can clearly conclude that the proclamation/our legal system gives enough consideration/recognition for communities knowledge and communities right over genetic resources and related traditional knowledge.

3.4.1.2. General provisions Objectives of the proclamation

The objective of this Proclamation is to ensure that the country and its communities obtain fair and equitable share from the benefits arising out of the use of genetic resources so as to promote the conservation and sustainable utilization of the country's biodiversity resources.[174]

The three main objectives of the CBD (conservation, sustainable use of biological diversity, and fair and equitable benefit sharing) are clearly seen in the above mentioned provision. The third paragraph of the preamble confirms the need to enact access legislation since the CBD requires so. [175]

Scope of applications

The proclamation applies to all kinds of access to genetic resources and community knowledge found in both *in situ* and *ex situ* conditions. Genetic resources found *in situ condition* are those found (on site) in the wild or on the

---

[173] See the six and seventh paragraphs of the preamble

[174] ABS proclamation, Article 3

[175] WHEREAS, Ethiopia is a part to the Convention on Biological Diversity and Convention requires the enactment of access legislation; The Preamble

farm.[176] *Ex situ* (off site) condition is genetic resource found in a gene bank outside its natural habitat.[177]

And *in-situ conservation* refers to the conservation of ecosystems and natural habitats and the maintenance and recovery of viable populations of species in their natural surroundings while *ex-situ conservation* refers to the conservation of components of biological diversity out-side their natural habitats.

This proclamation also doesn't apply to customary use and exchange of genetic resources or community knowledge by and among Ethiopian local communities and for direct consumption.[178]

3.4.1.2.1. Ownership of genetic resources and community knowledge

It is clear that there is international consensus as to some resources which are common heritage of mankind that is resources found on the sea bed and celestial bodies, but there was no consensus as to genetic/biological resources. Hence, one of the hated debates over the issue of biodiversity and bio-piracy is the issue of common heritage of mankind as opposed to the sovereign ownership of states over biological/genetic resources. The first internationally binding instrument to declare states' sovereign ownership over their biological resources is the CBD. In the fourth paragraph its preamble and subsequent provisions[179] the convention clearly provides that states have sovereign right over their own biological resources.

Coming to our legal system it reflects the same idea of the convention. The ownership of genetic resources shall be vested in the state and the Ethiopian people. It also recognizes the ownership of local communities over their traditional knowledge; *the ownership of community knowledge shall be vested in the concerned local community.*[180]

---

[176] ABS proclamation Article 2(7)

[177] ABS proclamation, Article 2 (4)

[178] ABS proclamation, Article 4

[179] See Articles 3, 15 (1), and the fourth paragraph of the preamble of CBD

[180] CBD, Article 5 (1) & (2)

3.4.1.2.2. Conditions of Access

What does access means? When we look at the convention which is the ground for the enactment of access to genetic resources and community knowledge and community right of Ethiopia, i.e. CBD, does not give a clear definition for the term access. But coming to our legal system, the proclamation provides a definition for the term 'access'. Article 2 (1) of the proclamation states that: unless the context requires otherwise "access" means the collection, acquisition, transfer or use of genetic resources and/or community knowledge.

A) Conditions of Access

"Each Contracting Party shall endeavor to create conditions to facilitate access to genetic resources ...."[181]; "Each Contracting Party shall take legislative, administrative or policy measures, as appropriate, with the aim that the private sector facilitates access.........."[182]

Looking at the above mentioned provisions and other relevant provisions of CBD; it is clear that member states are duty bound to provide legislative and policy measures to facilitate access to genetic resources. Accordingly our proclamation provides provisions describing how an individual or entity can get access to genetic resources of the country and community knowledge.

It is the concept of ownership of property that is also reflected on the ownership of states over their genetic resources. Whenever one is owner of a property others cannot posses/access, use or dispose the property without the permission of the owner. The same justification lay behind the sovereign ownership of states over their genetic resources. Both under the CBD and our proclamation it is clearly provided that states are owners of their genetic resources. Hence, by the principle of property, other states, individuals, and companies have no right to access or

---

[181] CBD, Article 15.2

[182] CBD, Article 16.4

utilize the genetic resources without the permission of owner states or without fulfilling the procedures that the owner states requires to be fulfilled before access or utilization. Some of the legal issues, of course the main one, which are addressed by the ABS proclamation and regulation are the legal requirements and procedures that should be followed before access and use of genetic resources, briefed as follows.

B) Access Permit

The article provides no person shall access genetic resources or community knowledge unless in possession of written access permit granted by the Institute based on prior informed consent.[183]

To get access to the genetic resources of the country and community knowledge one should necessarily get a document evidencing a written permission for access from the competent authority. As it is provided under ABS regulation 'Institute' refers to the Institute of Biodiversity Conservation established by Proclamation No. 120/98 (as amended). [184]In addition access permit to genetic resources shall not be construed to refer to permit to the related community knowledge and permit to access community knowledge should not also be taken as a permit to the genetic resource unless expressly provided otherwise. [185]In relation to movement of genetic resources out of Ethiopia one should get a special export permit. It states that *'no person shall export genetic resources out of Ethiopia unless in possession of export permit granted by the Institute to this effect.'[186]* This provision helps to tackle the easy movement of our biological/genetic resources out of our country.

The proclamation also requires any person to get permit from the institution even for exploration of genetic resources. As it is provided under part five of the proclamation no one is allowed to make exploration of genetic resources without

---

[183] ABS proclamation, Article 11 (1)

[184] ABS regulation, Article 2 (7)

[185] ABS proclamation, Article 11 (2)

[186] ABS proclamation, Article 11 (3)

exploration permit from the institute except organs of the state empowered by the law to conserve genetic resources. The section further provides the legal frame work of as to the procedure of acquiring exploration permit and rights and responsibilities of any explorer.[187]

C) Exceptions

There are some exceptions to the above listed conditions of access. Access for the customary use and exchange of genetic resources and community knowledge by and among Ethiopian Local communities and use of biological resources for direct consumption which doesn't involve use of genetic resources doesn't need a written access permit from the institute. In addition organs of state which are empowered by law to conserve genetic resources are not also expected to get a document showing a permit for access.[188]

3.4.1.2.3. Basic pre-conditions of permit

As has been mentioned many times above while discussing the Nagoya Protocol and the CBD; among the pre-requisites of access the basic[189] are the PIC (prior informed consent) and the MAT (mutually agreed terms). The proclamation also reflects the same requirements of prior informed consent as a precondition of access to genetic resources and to community knowledge. And any person who wants to obtain permit to access genetic resources or community knowledge shall present an application in writing to the Institute.[190] The other basic pre condition to get access permit is the fair and equitable sharing of benefits out of the utilization of genetic resources and community knowledge accessed. Looking at the specific provision dealing with the issue provides that *"The state and the concerned local community shall obtain fair and equitable share from benefits arising out of the*

---

[187] ABS proclamation, Articles 22-25

[188] ABS proclamation, Article 4 (1-4)

[189] Which are intended to tackle misappropriation or bio-piracy of genetic resources; though not effective

[190] Which are intended to tackle misappropriation or bio-piracy of genetic resources; though not effective

utilization of genetic resources and community knowledge accessed."[191] As we can see from the title of the article it deals with the 'basic pre-conditions' that needs to be fulfilled even before one gets access to any genetic resource or related community knowledge. However, the wording of the provision seems to address a scenario after an access obtained. It states *"The state and the concerned local community shall obtain fair and equitable share from benefits arising out of the utilization...."* It is impossible to put the obtaining of benefits arising from the utilization as a pre condition for access as utilization and benefit sharing are situations that come into picture after one already gets an access. Therefore, an effective way of addressing the problem of the provision would be to construe that the provision refers to MAT (mutually agreed terms) as to the benefit sharing that could be made with the state or the concerned local community. Taking the MAT is one precondition to get access is a better way in fighting up against bio-piracy and it is an approach taken by many countries and international instruments like Nagoya Protocol. In the proclamation, though not under the provision dealing with pre-requisites for permit, there is the concept of MAT. When we look at Article 14 (2) of the proclamation it states that *'Upon giving of prior informed consent, the Institute shall, based on the provisions of this proclamation, negotiate and conclude genetic resources access agreement.'* The provision clearly provides that an access agreement should be signed after securing a prior informed consent of the state or the concerned local community. But nowhere in the proclamation is found a clear provision dealing with MAT and providing it as a pre-requisite for access permit.

There are two more main basic requirements before access permit is granted; the first is if the an access applicant is a foreigner he/she/it should provide a letter of assurance of cooperation from his national state in implementing concerning applicants obligations of and if access is granted the collection of GR and CK shall be accompanied by a personnel from the institute or from a relevant institution to be assigned by the institute. [192]The other requirement is about researches conducted in relation to the GR or CK in consideration. The proclamation requires researches

---

[191] ABS proclamation, Article 12 (3)

[192] ABS proclamation, Article 12 (4)&(5)

should be conducted here in Ethiopia with the participation of Ethiopian nationals designated by the institute and if it is impossible it conduct it in Ethiopia; a letter of assurance as the compliance with the access obligations. [193]

3.4.1.2.4. Special Access Permit

The Institute may, without the need to strictly follow the access procedure provided for in this Proclamation, grant specific access permit to Ethiopia national public research and higher learning institutions and intergovernmental institutions based in the country, so that they have facilitated access to genetic resources and community knowledge for purpose of development and academic research activities they undertake within the country. Where the Institute grants specific access permits to such institutions, it shall determine, as appropriate, the obligations they shall assume while having access under such permit.[194]

3.4.1.2.5. Denial of Access

Access applications may be denied for any of the following reasons as provided under Article 13 of the proclamation. If the species for which an access application is made for an endangered species. The other ground of denial is if the access may have adverse effects upon human health or the cultural values of the local community; this is the justification of *ordre public and morality* which is discussed above. An access application could also be denied if it may cause undesirable impact on the environment or if it could cause loss of ecosystem. If an access is intended to use genetic resources for a purpose contrary to the national laws of Ethiopia or if there has been an experience of violating access agreements before on the applicant side; could be additional grounds to deny access to an application. [195]

The institute may even alter, suspend, terminate, put limitation on the size of

---

[193] ABS proclamation, Article 12 (6)&(7)

[194] ABS proclamation, Article 15 (1)

[195] ABS proclamation, Article 13

genetic resources to be accessed or put any other appropriate limitation on access for reasons provided by the proclamation. Such reasons include: if the access permit holder have violated or failed to comply with the provisions of the Proclamation or the terms and conditions of the access agreement or where the access causes risk of damage to genetic resources or the environment or affects overriding public interest or if there is an evidence of threat of genetic erosion or degradation of the environment.[196]

3.4.1.3. Access to Community Knowledge

Our proclamation gives recognition to community right over their genetic resources and community knowledge, the later is also mentioned as 'traditional knowledge' in many literatures. Community rights given recognition under the proclamation include the right to regulate the access to their community knowledge; an inalienable right to use their genetic resources and community knowledge; and the right to share from the benefit arising out of the utilization of their genetic resources and community knowledge.[197] The use right includes both the using of the genetic resource or the related traditional knowledge as per their practice and custom and exchange among themselves in the course of sustaining their livelihood as provided under Article 8 of the proclamation. The second sub article further mentions that no legal restriction shall be provided on this right and it is inalienable right of the community.

Coming to the right to regulate access to their community knowledge it includes the right to give PIC or deny PIC; or restrict an already given PIC whenever it could be detrimental to the integrity of their cultural or natural heritages or socio-life of the community and right to demand restriction or withdrawal of an already given PIC on their genetic resources by the institute.[198]

---

[196] (1-6) ABS proclamation, Article

[197] 21 ABS proclamation, Article 6

[198] ABS proclamation, Articles 7 and 8

3.4.1.3.1. Access procedures

The proclamation provides, under Article 14, that one should submit access application in order to get access to genetic resources and community knowledge. The first sub article of the same states that the conditions and procedures of the application to be provided by a regulation which is Regulation No. 169/2009. And the regulation divides access procedures into two broad categories as 'commercial access procedure' (Articles 3-10) and 'non-commercial access procedure' provided under Articles 11-13 of the regulation.

A) Commercial Access

First an access application shall be made to the institute, then admission and registration of access application will be made, as a subsequent step the institute will make an examination of the application as per the proclamation and Article 4 of the regulation and finally if the institute ascertains that there is sufficient ground to deny access denies the proposed access and communicates the same to the access applicant or if no ground to deny will give public notice of the access application.

Upon the expiry of the time limit given for objection and public opinion[199] and still if there is no ground to deny the access the institute will grant the access for the required genetic resource or community knowledge. [200]

B) Non Commercial Access

Non commercial access refers to those access applications made by Ethiopian higher learning and research institutions and also intergovernmental institutions based in Ethiopia. Upon application the institute stating the obligations may grant

---

[199] Thirty days after the publication of access application (see Article 6 (3) Council of Ministers Regulation to Provide for Access to Genetic Resources and Community Knowledge and Community Rights, Reg. No. 169/2009 Fed. Neg.Gaz., 15th year No.67,(hereinafter the ABS Regulation)

[200] ABS regulation, Articles 3-10

access to the applying institution. Unless there is a special permit and an access agreement the accessing institution shall have no right to export the resource accessed out Ethiopia. This is helpful provision in tackling improper exporting of genetic resources or community knowledge and to protect the interest of the country. [201]

3.4.1.4. Benefit Sharing

As we can read from the objective of the proclamation the main purpose of ensuring equitable sharing of benefits arising out of the utilization of the genetic resource is conservation and sustainable usage of the country's genetic resources. For instance, the same is reflected under Article 18 (2) of the proclamation. It states that *"The remaining portion of the monetary benefit from access to genetic resources, after deducting the share of the local community as determined pursuant to Article 9 (1) of this Proclamation, shall be allocated for conservation of biodiversity and the promotion of community knowledge......"* Article 18 is the main provision dealing with benefit sharing in the proclamation. However, it addresses only issue of benefit sharing between the state and the local community and how to utilize the monetary benefits are to be allocated for conservation and sustainable use. It never addresses the benefit sharing between the Ethiopian government/the institute or local communities on the one hand and any other accessing organization or individual is regulated. This is one of the lope holes of our legislation and might create a problem in addressing issues related with benefit sharing. [202]The subsequent provision (Article 19) states the types of benefits (which includes both monetary and non- monetary) and the provision uses the word '**may**' which could be an indication that the list is not exhaustive and the last sub-article also creates a room for other forms of benefits since it reads 'Any other benefit as appropriate'.

---

[201] ABS regulation, Articles 11-13

[202] ABS proclamation, Article 18

3.4.1.5. Benefit sharing of local communities

Article 9 of the proclamation is specially designated to deal local communities right to share benefit. After recognizing the community's right to share benefits arising from utilization the second sub-article states that the community shall have the right to obtain 50% of the monetary benefit and shall be used for the common advantages of the concerned local community[203] as regulated by the regulation. [204]

3.4.1.6. Institutional Regime of ABS

There are seven different institutions that will take part in the implementation of ABS or this proclamation. These stakeholder institutions include Ministry of Agriculture and Rural Development, Institute of Biodiversity Conservation, Local Communities as one stakeholder customary institution, Regional Bodies, Customs Office, Mail Service Institutions and Quarantine Control Institutions.

A) The ministry of agriculture and rural development is responsible for the implementation of the provisions of the proclamation related with genetic resources of wild animals.[205]

B) The Institute of Biodiversity and Conservation

Powers and duties of the Institute

A) Follow up and ensuring the access agreement is carried out as agreed and as per the pertinent legal provisions. The institute conducts the execution by inspection, periodic progress and status report by access permit holders and the relevant institutions designated to accompany the collection, participate in the research and monitor the implementation of access agreement and a report by any

---

[203] ABS proclamation, Article 9

[204] ABS regulation, Articles 28 and the following

[205] ABS proclamation, Article 26

other individual or other mechanism deemed appropriate.[206]

B) Collect the benefits to be obtained from access agreements and pass over to beneficiaries. The beneficiaries, for instance, might be the local communities; as it is mentioned under Article 9 of the proclamation the communities have the right to share 50% of any monetary benefit of the utilization of their genetic resources. Therefore, this is obviously the responsibility of the institute.[207]

C) Cause that legal actions are taken against offences committed in violations of this Proclamation. In violation of this proclamation means in effect any offensive activity in accessing genetic material or related community knowledge or in conservation or benefit sharing. Therefore, the institute is duty bound to ensure proper accessing of genetic resources and benefit sharing as well.[208]

D) Other duties of the institute include preparing model access agreements, collect, analyze and as necessary disseminate to users information on access to genetic resources and community knowledge, issue directives and perform such other activities necessary for the implementation of this Proclamation, and delegate its powers and duties to other legally established bodies; where deemed necessary and convenient to carry out its duties in a better way.[209]

C) Local communities

Local communities are recognized as one of the customary institution in our legal system and even internationally. Therefore, the concerned communities are main stakeholders and participants in the issues related with ABS. Hence, the proclamation provides some responsibilities of local communities. The main duty of local communities is fighting improper acts of access to genetic resource or related community knowledge. The proclamation provides that:

---

[206] ABS proclamation, Article 27 (1) & 20 (1)
[207] ABS proclamation, Article 27 (2)

[208] ABS proclamation, Article 27 (6)
[209] ABS proclamation, Article 27 (3),(5),(6), (7) &

"prohibit any person, who does not belong to their communities, from collecting or taking genetic resources from their localities without having the necessary permit; and

"require any person, who does not belong to their communities and who is collecting or taking genetic resource from their localities, to show his access permit, and if he is without permit immediately notify or present him to the nearest kebele or wereda administration;"[210]

D) Regional bodies

Regional bodies like kebeles, weredas and other relevant regional organizations are entrusted with the responsibility that is also given to local communities. The only difference is regional bodies are required to regulate that genetic resources are not accessed from their jurisdiction without access permit and to require a permit from anyone who doesn't belong to the community. [211]

E) Customs Offices

Customs offices are government institutions which play a vital role in any in and out going transactions and commodities. Hence, the role of this office is more important in avoiding the illegal exporting of genetic resources out of Ethiopia. Accordingly, Article 30 provides the duties of the customs office to be inspecting that any genetic resources being taken out of the country has been accompanied with an export permit given by the Institute and require any person leaving the country who is transporting or is in possession of genetic resource to produce the necessary permit to this effect from the Institute as the main duties of the office.[212]

---

[210] (8) ABS proclamation, Article 28 (1-2)

[211] ABS proclamation, Article 29

[212] ABS proclamation, Article 30

F) Mail Service Institutions

Mail service institutions are other institutions which could possibly take part in the process of tackling the illegal outgoing of our genetic resources. So it is a right move to consider such institutions as part takers in the fighting bio-piracy as genetic resource could also be exported in the form of mail. The provision requires that:

"Postal and other courier service institutions shall, before receiving and transporting genetic resources out of the country as mail require their clients to produce permit from the Institute to export the genetic resources out of the country."[213]

G) Quarantine Control Institutions

The last institution which is considered by the proclamation to take part in the processes of ensuring proper ABS is the Quarantine control Institution. Article 32 states the responsibility of such institutions as follows:

"Quarantine control Institution shall, ensure that the quarantine certificate they issue to biological resource products, contain a statement indicating that the certificate does not constitute a permit to use the product as genetic resource and that doing so is prohibited and would constitute an offence."[214]

3.4.1.7. Penalty

The offences for which the proclamation provides penalties for can be categorized into the following two broad categories: violations against provisions of the proclamation and violations against ABS agreement. And the following are lists of possible violations listed under Article 35 and the following provisions;

---

[213] ABS proclamation, Article 31

[214] ABS proclamation, Article 32

Accessing genetic resources or community knowledge without access permit

Providing false information during access application or subsequent stages

Changing the purpose for which the resource is accessed without the permission of the institute after acquiring access permit

Exploring genetic resources without exploration permit from the institute

For the above listed violations the following measures can be taken as a punishment or a corrective measure:

Confiscation of the genetic resource accessed in violation

Cancellation of access permit granted. This is applicable where there is violation of an access agreement by the access permit holder.

Civil liability equivalent to the damage caused due to the violation

Criminal liability could also arise from such kind of violations; and it could be a rigorous imprisonment not less than three years and a fine of not less than ten-thousand and not exceeding thirty-thousand birr.

If the offence is committed in relation to genetic resources endemic to Ethiopia

"The punishment shall be, depending of the circumstance, rigorous imprisonment of not less than five years and not exceeding twelve-years and a fine ranging from fifty thousand birr to hundred-thousand birr."

"Where the offences under this Article are committed in negligence, the penalty shall be a fine of not less than five thousand birr or, depending on the circumstance and the gravity of the offence, simple imprisonment of not less than

three months."[215]

3.5. The Ethiopian Legal Regime as compared to the Nagoya Protocol

The Nagoya Protocol is a landmark achievement in the international governance of biodiversity. As a protocol to the CBD, it serves as an instrument containing a national and international framework for implementation of the CBD's access and benefit sharing provisions.[216] Africa had for many years demanded for a legally binding international instrument aimed at regulating access to genetic resources, their products and derivatives and also an instrument that would ensure the protection of the traditional knowledge, innovations and practices of indigenous and local communities under benefit-sharing agreements to prevent further exploitation and misappropriation of its biological and genetic resources.[217] Therefore, the Nagoya Protocol, though is full of many compromises on the interest of Africans', is considered as a better solution to fight against bio-piracy and misappropriation of their resources.

Fair and equitable sharing of benefits is one of the key objectives of the CBD. The Nagoya Protocol is simply the further negotiation of this third objective of the CBD. Reading of the preamble of the protocol states that:

"Recalling that the fair and equitable sharing of benefits arising from the utilization of genetic resources is one of three core objectives of the Convention, and recognizing that this Protocol pursues the implementation of this objective within the Convention,"[218]

---

[215] ABS proclamation, Articles 33-35

[216] Koutouki, cited above at note 101, p 1

[217] Mafuratidze R., Critical Review of the Nagoya Protocol on Access & Benefit Sharing: Analysis of its Provisions Against the African Model Law and Possibilities for its Implementation at National Level, p 2, Available on http://www.ctdt.co.zw/attachments/079_NAGOYA%20PROTOCOL.pdf, Accessed on [December, 12/12]

[218] See the first paragraph of the preamble of the Nagoya Protocol

Looking at Article 5 (2) of the Nagoya Protocol it provides responsibility of member states in ensuring the achievement of the above mentioned objective of the protocol.

Art. 5 (2):-

"Each Party shall take legislative, administrative or policy measures, as appropriate, with the aim of ensuring that benefits arising from the utilization of genetic resources that are held by indigenous and local communities, in accordance with domestic legislation regarding the established rights of these indigenous and local communities over these genetic resources, are shared in a fair and equitable way with the communities concerned, based on mutually agreed terms."

The most important advances of the protocol are clear legal frameworks and a guideline on how to design national provisions on ABS. Therefore, in order to see the relevance of our legal system in fighting against bio-piracy it is appropriate to compare our ABS regime with the most recent and said to be better accommodating the interest of Africans; which is the Nagoya Protocol. Once a state designs and implements a well regulated access and benefit sharing regime it is easier to tackle acts of pirates. Therefore, when we look in contrast most of the provisions of under our ABS regime are similar with that of the protocols'. In terms of time since the protocol is legislated after the coming into force of our ABS regime; our system is not designed in reference of the protocol which in effect brings some discrepancies. I will mention some elements of the Nagoya Protocol that should be introduced to our legal system in the recommendation part of this paper.

Chapter Four

4. Conclusion and Recommendation

Biological diversities and genetic resources are important for the life of human being on earth and are one of the pillar sources of sustainable development and food security for the world as a whole. Biological diversity may be defined as the variation present in all species of plants and animals, their genetic material and the ecosystems in which they occur while 'genetic diversity' refers to the heritable variation within and between populations of organisms and plant species.[219] As per the definition given by CBD; the biological diversity may include all ecosystem, plant, animal species, and genetic resources.[220] Genetic Resources provide a huge wealth of resources for the development of biotechnology as a basis of innovation. Genetic resources are sometimes called the "first resource" of the natural resources on this planet the others being land, air, and water. Genes are the link from generation to generation of all living matter. Therefore, attention to genetic resources means attention to the vast diversity among and between species of animals, plants, and microorganisms.[221]

However, the issue of ownership of genetic resources and any related TK has been and is one of the most controversial issues internationally. There are two major lines of arguments; the first one is the common heritage argument which proposes that biological and genetic resources are common heritages of mankind; hence there should be no restriction of ownership. The second line of argument, however, recognizes the sovereign right and ownership of states over their genetic resources.

Until the 1990s companies involved in activities of accessing the genetic

---

[219] Rao R. V., et al, <u>Genetic diversity and conservation and utilization of plant genetic resources</u>, (2002), Kluwer Acadamic Publisher, Netherlands, pp 1-2

[220] CBD, Article 2

[221] Genetic Resources Conservation Program Annual Report, Report No. 1, University of California Genetic Resources Conservation Program, Available on http://grcp.ucdavis.edu/publications/doc1/R1Body.pdf, Accessed on [December 17/2012]

resources or related traditional knowledge of biodiversity rich countries (mostly the developing countries) without the permission and proper compensation made for the owner state or local community. Bio-piracy is the word which was later coined for this act of plundering genetic resources. However, this regime of free access changed when the Convention on Biological Diversity

(CBD) was adopted in 1992 to curb alarming rates of biodiversity loss and to "ensure that the discrepancy between resource provider and the technology developer became more balanced" [222]

One of the agenda which further triggered the debate over ownership of genetic resources is the issue of patenting of life forms.[223]

Conventional wisdom treats biodiversity and biotechnology as rivalrous values. The global south is home to most of earth's vanishing species, while the global north holds the capital and technology needed to develop this natural wealth. The south argues that intellectual property laws enable pharmaceutical companies and seed breeders in the industrialized north to commit bio-piracy. By contrast, the United States has characterized calls for profit-sharing as a threat to the global life sciences industry. Both sides magnify the dispute, on the apparent consensus that commercial exploitation of genetic resources holds the key to biodiversity conservation.[224]

In 1995, the World Trade Organization (WTO) developed an agreement outlining Trade-Related aspects of Intellectual Property Rights, known as the

---

[222] Afreen Sh., et al, Bio-prospecting: Promoting and Regulating Access to Genetic Resources and Benefit Sharing, (2008), kalkota india, Indian Institute of Management Calcutta Working Paper Series WPS No. 631, p 3

[223] What is mostly done by international pharmaceuticals is that they just explore a genetic resource and will make some innovations upon the naturally existing genetic makeup and will apply for the patenting of the innovation they made to the already existing genetic resource. Then by the rule of patent everyone is excluded from the usage of a patented property. This in effect excludes both the owner state and owner local community, in case of community knowledge, and is mostly done without any compensation for the provider state. This is what the developing countries label as bio-piracy and striving to fight it.

[224] Jim Ch., Bio-prospect Theory, Available on http://poseidon01.ssrn.com/delivery.php?IDSSRnpdf, Accessed on [November 16/2012]

TRIPS Agreement, which is a comprehensive multilateral agreement concerning intellectual property. As laid out in its preamble, the TRIPS Agreement aims at attempting "to reduce distortions and impediments to international trade, and taking into account the need to pro-mote effective and adequate protection of intellectual property rights, and to ensure that measures and procedures to enforce intellectual property rights do not themselves become barriers to legitimate trade. The primary objective of the TRIPS Agreement is to promote access to and the transfer of technological innovations, and, at the same time, balance the rights and obligations of those producing and using biotechnology against social and economic concerns. Countries that sign the TRIPS Agreement agree to grant patents for any invention, both for products and processes, in all technology fields without discrimination i.e. including innovations conducted in relation to genetic resources, subject to standard requirements, including the requirements that the invention be novel and industrially applicable.

The core of the international debate revolving around the issue is hence, the global north are for the patenting of life forms since, they claim that, it is an incentive for the innovations related with genetic resources while the global south are lined up on the contrary claiming that patenting is simply a mechanism developed by the industrially developed ones' to get access to monopoly and private ownership over our genetic resources and related knowledge.

As far as the concept and practice of patent exist, as it is intrinsic to Intellectual Property, it will remain to be a treat to the genetic resources of the developing and bio-diverse countries.[225] And the available means of reducing its adverse effect is a well regulated regime and internationally binding requirements and guidelines.

It is provided under the CBD and an international consensus is reached that there should be PIC and MAT between the provider state/local community and the user entity/person. The main problem, however, was the issue of compliance. How mandatorily could these requirements be observed or will effectively be complied by every stake-holders and mainly the north and big international pharmaceuticals?

---

[225] Gemedo Dale (Ph.D,), Director of the Institute of Biodiversity and Conservation

is the main question.

Since the ratification of the CBD many national and regional efforts have been made to operationalize its principles and regulate access to genetic resources and benefit sharing (ABS).

Among efforts made so far the Nagoya Protocol on Access to Genetic Resources and the Fair and Equitable Sharing of Benefits Arising from their Utilization is the most important and most recent. The main aim of the Nagoya Protocol, which adopted at the tenth meeting of the Conference of the Parties (COP 10) to the CBD held in Nagoya; is to ensure the fair and equitable sharing of benefits arising out of the utilization of genetic resources through greater legal certainty and transparency for both providers and users of the genetic resources. The other main objective and importance as well of the Nagoya Protocol is that it tries to provide internationally binding legal guideline which countries should incorporate using legislative and administrative measures and which user and provider states should follow in ABS agreement.

4.1. The Importance of Nagoya Protocol

The Nagoya Protocol has a significant importance in the following main areas:

One of the importances of the protocol is that it helps, to both provider and user states, in putting a guideline predictable and uniform legal regime in the access and benefit sharing process.

The protocol obliges member states to legislate their laws in conformity with the ABS provisions of the protocol. It states that Each Party shall take legislative, administrative or policy measures, as appropriate, in order that the benefits arising from the utilization of traditional knowledge associated with genetic resources are shared in a fair and equitable way with indigenous and local communities holding such knowledge.[226] The importance of this obligation on member states is in

---

[226] Nagoya Protocol, Article 5 (2)

facilitating the access process for user countries and in creating a predictable access procedure in every member state and also in creating a better secured way of getting their benefits from their GRs and related TK of the bio-diverse states or the provider states.

The other importance of the protocol is that; since it requires member states to provide for a means of judicial process in their legal system and in their mutual agreement. Article 18 states that; Each Party shall ensure that an opportunity to seek recourse is available under their legal systems, consistent with applicable jurisdictional requirements, in cases of disputes arising from mutually agreed terms.

It is helpful, for countries like Ethiopia and other mega diverse states, in fighting misappropriation or bio-piracy of genetic resources and related traditional knowledge.

4.2.   Failures of the Protocol

The expectation of developing countries form the Nagoya Protocol was very high. One of their expectations was to get a solution to resolve the problem of bio-piracy. The solution that the developing countries were expecting is the amendment of the TRIPs agreement, which was proposed by group of countries. The amendment proposed is the inclusion of the **'disclosure requirement'**[227] in the IP legal regime of the WTO which is the TRIPs. However, this interest of the developing countries was not included in the Nagoya Protocol. Instead of the disclosure requirement a compromise was reached; that was the establishment of **'check points'** to monitor whether PIC, MAT and other legal requirements of the provider state is fulfilled before accessing a genetic resource or related traditional

---

[227] The disclosure requirement proposes that the TRIPS Agreement should be amended in order to require that an applicant for a patent relating to biological materials or to traditional knowledge shall provide, as a condition to acquiring patent rights: disclosure of the source and country of origin of the biological resource and of the traditional knowledge used in the invention; evidence of prior informed consent through approval of authorities under the relevant national regimes; and evidence of fair and equitable benefit sharing under the national regime of the country of origin. The TRIPS-CBD Issue in the WTO: A South Asian Perspective, Available on http://cutsgrc.org/pdf/CUTS_GRC_Note_on_TRIPS-CBD_Issues, Accessed on [November 16, 2012]

knowledge.

This leaves open the possibility for countries to require **'patent office'** be designated as a check point. The checkpoint option is a **'weak alternative'** to a proper disclosure requirement, since countries have wide latitude in designating their checkpoints. The Nagoya Protocol does not include a list of mandatory checkpoints, among which many biodiversity-rich developing countries had proposed the inclusion of patent offices. [228] However, it is still the first binding obligation (if signed by 50 countries) to ensure access and benefit sharing of genetic resources and related traditional knowledge. This strengthens the effort to fight bio-piracy one more step stronger than it was before.

The other problem of the protocol is its weak wording in legislating the provisions. Most the words/ phrases are loosely tuned and giving much more discretion for each member state. For instance we find the following phrases frequently in most of the provision of the protocol; **'each party shall take measures as appropriate'** and **'shall take the necessary step as appropriate'**. It is very subjective what amounts 'appropriate' or 'necessary measure' in different countries according to the different contributing factors and the kind of policy they follow. Such approach gives a very wide playing ground to deviate from the protocol and weakens the compliance of it.

The main failure of Nagoya Protocol, however, is that there are no specific compliance provisions if the user company fails to comply with the MAT/the benefit sharing agreement. The other drawback of this protocol is that it doesn't extend the above mentioned requirements for TK.

4.3. Does Ethiopia benefit from NP?

As it has been mentioned above; though the NP didn't achieved the interest which was presented by the developing countries a stronger compliance measure, like the disclosure requirement, it is a step forward in the fight against bio-piracy

---

[228] Cited above at note 97

and establishing internationally accepted binding guideline of ABS of genetic resources and related community knowledge. This is helpful for Ethiopia as it is for any other developing genetic resource rich countries in the world. The protocol will also help our country in revising its ABS regime so that it better protect our genetic resource and community knowledge.

The protocol also puts an obligation on the parties to cooperate in capacity building. The capacity building is mainly aimed at helping parties which are developing, least developed, small island developing states and states with economies in transition in capacity development and strengthening of human resources and institutional capacities to effectively implement this Protocol.[229] In support of the implementation of this Protocol,

"capacity-building and development may address, inter alia, the following key areas: Capacity to implement, and to comply with the obligations of, this Protocol; Capacity to negotiate mutually agreed terms; Capacity to develop, implement and enforce domestic legislative, administrative or policy measures on access and benefit-sharing; and Capacity of countries to develop their endogenous research capabilities to add value to their own genetic resources."[230]

Support of legal and institutional measures, as provided under 22.5 (a) of the protocol, are also the other areas where capacity building measures should be given by developed parties.

As Ethiopia is one of the least developed countries all the above capacity buildings expected from the developed ones' will be beneficial for our country.

Therefore, it is clear that, given the proper implementation of the protocol and observance of parties accordingly, the Nagoya Protocol is has a wide range benefits to strengthen our legal and institutional regime of ABS and in fighting against bio-piracy as well.

---

[229] Nagoya Protocol Article 22

[230] Ibid

4.4. Is our system (legal & institutional) well regulated to fight bio-piracy?

To check whether our legal and institutional regime is well regulated or not there should be a reference. This work took mainly the Nagoya Protocol and other related international regimes too as a point of reference. In light of institutional regimes, in addition to the protocol, best experience of some other countries is considered as a reference.

The legal aspect of our ABS regime is more or less similar with the provisions of Nagoya Protocol, other states' ABS regime and model laws on access and benefit sharing. However, the main point is the issue of compliance and the capacity of ensuring proper implementation of the already existing provisions. In most cases the capacity of a state (economic, political and social levels of development) is critical in the proper implementation of a legal regime. Therefore, in order to make the effective implementation of our ABS regime capacity building is crucial. In addition; to further strengthen our ABS regime and to make our system a more prudently regulated legal regime, especially in fighting against bio-piracy, the researcher recommends the introduction and/or amendment of the following legal and institutional mechanisms.

4.4.1. Model Agreement on Access and Benefit Sharing of Genetic Resources of Ethiopia

The model agreement is a readymade contractual terms providing the details of the agreement that is signed between Ethiopia and any accessing entity. The model agreement has fifteen parts some of the core parts are: parties to the agreement describe the contracting parties of the agreement and their detailed address. The Institute of Biodiversity and Conservation (IBC) is provided as a contracting party representing Ethiopia, as it provided in the proclamation. Scope of access and obligations of the parties describes the type and place of the biological/genetic resource accessed and the amount allowed to be accessed and for what specific purposes the resource is allowed. Intellectual property ownership; this part deals with issues of IP specifically mentioning that the company shall neither claim nor obtain IP rights and any inventions are mentioned jointly. Transfer to third parties;

115

this part also clearly provides that without the clear permission of Ethiopia that the company cannot transfer the biological/genetic resource to third party. Benefit sharing clearly stipulating both monetary and non monetary benefits. Other parts include ownership and confidentiality, amendments, duration of the agreement, penalty, termination, dispute settlement, guarantee, applicable laws, language of communication, monitoring and follow up, and entry into force of the agreement. See the ANNEX for the full version of the agreement.

4.5.   Recommendations

In order to fight bio-piracy from its root internationally binding measures should be taken. The only possible and potentially effective method is to revise provisions is of the TRIPS (Art 27.3) as it is binding among WTO member countries. The TRIPS agreement must include the following requirements as pre-requisite before a patent is granted on genetic resource and/or related traditional knowledge and also must require member states to the WTO to include in their national legislations.

(i)   Disclosure of the source and country of origin of the biological resource and of the traditional knowledge used in the invention;

(ii)   Evidence of prior informed consent through approval of authorities under the relevant national regimes;

(iii)   Evidence of fair and equitable benefit sharing under the national regime of the country of origin; and

(iv)   Grounds of invalidation or appeal for patents granted improperly

Therefore if all member states to WTO include such requirement into their national legislations it could be easy any act of theft of genetic resource.

The second is reconciling the inconsistency between CBD and the TRIPs agreements. The major inconsistencies can be summarized as follows:

CBD recognizes national states sovereign rights of ownership over their biological resources while TRIPs doesn't recognize so and requires patenting of biological resources.

The CBD provides that appropriate benefit-sharing is to occur when biological resources are utilized, while TRIPs does not call for any appropriate allocation of benefits between the provider of materials and the holder of the patent.

The CBD calls for prior informed consent before receiving access to the biological resources of a given state, while TRIPs does not recognize such a necessity of consent.

The CBD gives greater weight to public interest and community possessions than private property and private interests, while TRIPs does exactly the opposite.

Therefore, the TRIPs should be revised in a way it incorporates the objectives and requirements provided under CBD in order to fight bio-piracy in a better way.

The first of my recommendations in light of our legal system is that; our legal regime should be revised in a way it puts the provisions of the Nagoya Protocol on the ground which in effect needs the amendment of our legal regime in light of the protocol. Therefore, I recommend that the inclusion of the following provision helps to strengthen our ABS regime which in effect helps us in fighting against bio-piracy activities over our biological and genetic resources and related traditional/community knowledge.

A) Derivatives

The Nagoya Protocol is the first in defining 'derivatives' in including them under the ambit of the protection of the protocol. As per the protocol 'derivative' means a naturally occurring biochemical compound resulting from the genetic expression or metabolism of biological or genetic resources, even if it does not contain functional units of heredity.[231] The ABS laws of Ethiopia defines derivatives as *"man's product extracted or developed from biological resources, this may include products such as plant varieties, oils, resins, gums, chemicals and proteins"*[232]

Though the two definitions seem contradictory, they are parallel. The first definition states about naturally occurring biochemical compounds whereas the second about man's products extracted from biological resources. However, the Ethiopia's definition convenes slightly different message in that it includes products developed artificially (synthesized products) such as plant varieties and

chemicals from biological resources and this needs adjustment. Derivatives are the most important raw materials in industrial production of medicines, food, cosmetics, etc. and this definition will highly reinforce domestic laws of Ethiopia.[233]

B) Trans-boundary cooperation

This is a provision intended to address situations where a given in situ genetic resource found within the territory of more than one party.

1. "In instances where the same genetic resources are found in situ within the territory of more than one Party, those Parties shall endeavor to cooperate, as appropriate, with the involvement of indigenous and local communities concerned, where applicable, with a view to implementing this Protocol.

2. Where the same traditional knowledge associated with genetic resources is shared by one or more indigenous and local communities in several Parties, those Parties shall endeavor to cooperate, as appropriate, with the involvement of the indigenous and local communities concerned, with a view to implementing the

---

[231] Nagoya Protocol, Article 2 (e)

[232] ABS proclamation, Article 2 (3)

[233] Ethiopian Flora Network, Available at http://www.lbc.gov.et

objective of this Protocol" [234]

This article is not incorporated in the ABS laws of Ethiopia and needs serious consideration as we share similar genetic resources and associated indigenous knowledge with our neighbors such as Kenya, Sudan, Somalia and Eritrea which are parties to the CBD. [235]

C) Clearing House

Developing countries' main issue during the negotiation and one of the main challenges they were and are facing is the issue of compliance. They wanted user countries to have provisions in their legislation which monitor against misappropriation in support of compliance; this would be primarily in the form of a disclosure requirement, checkpoints and certificates of compliance.

The inclusion of disclosure requirement was not possible. The compromise reached on was the inclusion of PIC and MAT as mandatory prerequisites of access. To support compliance, Article 17 of the Nagoya Protocol requires parties to designate one or more check points that would receive information related to PIC, MATs and the source and utilization of the genetic resource. [236] A permit will be evidenced by the decision of a country to grant PIC and establish MAT; and of the fact that the resource has been accessed in compliance with the legal requirements of a country. The permit also forms the basis of an internationally recognized certificate. Once the permit is made available to the ABS Clearing House, it automatically acquires the status of international certificate. [237] So the Clearing House mechanism is provided under Article 14 of the Nagoya Protocol to further strengthen the compliance measures. The mechanism also helps to monitor

---

[234] Nagoya protocol, Article 11 (1-2)

[235] Cited above at note 146

[236] Mafuratidze, cited above at note 202, pp 16-17

[237] Nijar G., "Technical Brie: The Nagoya Protocol on Access and Benefit-Sharing of Genetic Resources: analysis and implementation options for developing countries", South Centre, Research Paper , vol. no. 36, (2010), IUCN, p 16

the utilization of genetic resource.

The ABS legal regime of Ethiopia again lacks to include the Clearing House mechanism as one form of ensuring the compliance in its access and benefit sharing regime. As it is also indicated under Article 18 (3) of the CBD and also under the Nagoya Protocol our legal system should also include the Clearing House system in its legislation; so that it is also harmonized with the protocol.

D) Awareness Raising

Article 21 of the NP states that

"Each Party shall take measures to raise awareness of the importance of genetic resources and traditional knowledge associated with genetic resources, and related access and benefit-sharing issues."

Looking at Article 18 of the CBD it even requires member states the inclusion of issues related with biodiversity in educational programs as a means of awareness raising. [238]

Looking at some of the experiences of Ethiopia on access and benefit sharing; the country has lost many benefits that it should have got due to many contributing factors. Partly, however, lack enough awareness one the main contributing factors for our loss. When we look at the way our endemic crop 'Teff' is accessed and how we finally lost control over it is caused due to lack of awareness on our part. Especially when we look at local communities of Ethiopia, whom most of them are holders of community knowledge, are not well educated lacks awareness on issues related with the importance of genetic resources and related community knowledge and the most dangerous treat to the resource which bio-piracy. Therefore,

---

[238] Contracting parties shall promote and encourage understanding of the importance of, and the measures required for, the conservation of biological diversity, as well as its propagation through media, and the inclusion of these topics inn educational programs; and cooperation as appropriate, with other states and international organizations in developing educational and public awareness programs, with respect to conservation and sustainable use of biological diversity. CBD, Article 18

awareness rising should be one the policy directions that our country should follow in fighting up against bio-piracy and the inclusion of it in the ABS legislation should be the first step in doing so. The awareness raising system should be designed to encompass all possible stakeholders; the society at large, researchers, academicians, local communities, stakeholders institutions and local authorities.

E) Code of Conduct, Guidelines and Best practice

Article 20 of the NP requires parties to encourage the development, update and use of voluntary code of conduct, guidelines and best practices in relation to access and benefit sharing. This helps to develop and strengthen the ABS legal regime more; hence better to include it in our ABS legislations.

Concerning **benefit sharing;** our ABS regime needs some amendments. Article 18 of the proclamation is the main provision dealing with benefit sharing. It states as follows: *(1) "the kind and the amount of the benefit to be shared by the state and local communities from access to genetic resources or community knowledge shall be determined case by case in each specific access agreements to be signed."*

(2) "The sharing of non-monetary benefits from access to genetic resources among the state and the concerned local community shall be......" Looking at the wording of the provision it deals only with the benefit sharing among the state and the concerned local community. This being as it is however, the regime should also entertain issues of benefit sharing between/ among the state or local community and accessing body

Many parts of its provision our legal *system* mentions that the state or concerned local community shall get the benefit from the utilization of genetic resources and related community knowledge. And access by a user state or company should also be made upon acquiring access permit. The Nagoya Protocol having same principle, but always mentions mutually agreed terms (MAT) as essential element of securing the benefit sharing. For instance Article 5 of the protocol dealing with fair and equitable sharing that is fair and equitable sharing

121

must be established between provider and the user. It further states that such sharing shall be upon mutually agreed terms.[239] Another provision; Article 7 of the protocol dealing with access to traditional knowledge related with genetic resources it again provides the MAT as one of the conditions for access agreement. It states that *".........traditional knowledge associated with genetic resources that is held by indigenous and local communities is accessed with the prior and informed consent or approval and involvement of these indigenous and local communities, and that mutually agreed terms have been established."[240]* In addition Article 13 also states providing information on PIC, MAT including benefit sharing as the responsibility of national focal points. In all above cases the protocol provides MAT as a means of implementing benefit sharing and sometimes as a precondition for access (Article 7).

When we look at our ABS regime, it only states that there should be fair and equitable benefit sharing from the utilization of genetic resources or related community knowledge. Mutually agreed term is nowhere mentioned both in the proclamation and regulation. Therefore, including MAT as a means of as one requirement that should be fulfilled to secure benefit sharing and access in some cases in our legal regime will be helpful in avoiding danger of losing benefits from access agreement which in effect helps fighting bio-piracy.

Concerning the model agreement; it is well regulated in a way that addresses every relevant issues related with access to our biological/genetic resources. From the experience on 'Teff', however, it is better to include the following amendments to the agreement.

On part 12 of the agreement, Termination, 12.2. provides that the agreement shall terminate upon court declaration of bankruptcy. The same provision was incorporated on the 'Teff' agreement, however the company never informed the

---

[239] In accordance with Article 15, paragraphs 3 and 7 of the Convention, benefits arising from the utilization of genetic resources as well as subsequent applications and commercialization shall be shared in a fair and equitable way with the Party providing such resources that is the country of origin of such resources or a Party that has acquired the genetic resources in accordance with the Convention. ***Such sharing shall be upon mutually agreed terms.*** (the the underlined statement), Nagoya Protocol, Article 5(1)

[240] Nagoya Protocol, Article 7

whole process before court decision which has created information gap for Ethiopia and also gave the company the chance to transfer the inventions to other companies before Ethiopia take any measure. Therefore, a provision that requires the contracting party to inform any application or process at court for declaration of bankruptcy should be communicated to the other party at the most earlier possible time before the final decision of the court.

Again taking lesson from the problems we faced in relation to the 'Teff' agreement an amendment should be made to the monitoring and follow-up part of the agreement. 17.3. provides that "the provider/Ethiopia has the right to review at any moment, through an independent account if it so wishes, the book keeping as well as the relevant administrative details of the items covered by this agreement." I recommend that this right of review of book keeping should extend too review of the proper implementation of the agreement itself on different issues covered by the agreement. For instance whether the biological/genetic resource accessed is being used only for the purpose agreed by the parties or not. On the case of 'Teff' there was no a check as to the implementation of the agreement from time to time. There was no information on the part of Ethiopia as to patenting over 'Teff' that the company acquired which is not of course part of the agreement. Therefore, there should be a provision requiring the parties to check the proper implementation of the agreement with a given interval of time.

4.5.1. Institutional amendments

For our institutional regime to work better in fighting improper access and misappropriation of genetic resources; creating a single body comprised of experts from all institutions or any form of networked system in which all stakeholder institutions are equally informed and work together in the process of bio-prospecting applications and access and benefit sharing procedure is important. For instance in Philippines there is a committee called *'The Inter Agency Committee'*. The main purpose of the committee is to use a multi stake-holder approach working to coordinate process of bio-prospecting applications and access and benefit sharing procedure and to discuss related institutional and political issues.[241]

Therefore, any similar kind of approach which involves all the listed stake-holder institution in ABS process, listed in the proclamation, is very helpful in fighting against bio-piracy and securing the proper implementation of the ABS regime of Ethiopia.

We need a special focus group! For instance, one of the main causes for the lose over our genetic resource of 'Teff' is lack of cooperation between the IBC and the Ethiopian IP office. On the ABS proclamation the mandate to negotiate and sign agreements including follow ups and compliance measures of ABS of genetic resource and related TK is fully given to the IBC without leaving any room for the IP office. The IBC lacks expertise as compared to the IP office. Therefore, there should be a common forum comprised of experts from both the IBC and the IP office which works together at the time of request for ABS agreement on our genetic resources.

The industrial sector of the country working on researches and pharmaceuticals are not considered as stakeholders in our ABS regime. It is much easier and effective to control activities of domestic industries and domestic pharmaceuticals than foreign ones' on activities related with access and benefit sharing and utilization of genetic resources. Therefore, first of all our ABS regime should consider the domestic industry working on this area and also should encourage them to involve on research and bio-prospecting activities since it is more easier to monitor.

In our ABS legal regime doesn't clearly mentions the possible stake-holders in the area of biodiversity as whole. Looking at the experience of some other states pioneer in legislating ABS regimes shows that there are listed stake-holders. Mostly mentioned stake-holders are state, local and indigenous communities, scientific institutions, representatives of the industrial sector, and NGOs. The above listed and other possible stake-holders, if any, should be referred in the ABS

---

[241] Smagadi A., "National Measures on Access to Genetic Resources and Benefit Sharing, The Case of Philippines", LEAD Journal, vol. 1/1,(2005), p 62, Available http://www.lead-journal.org/content/05050.pdf

regime of Ethiopia.

The establishment of national focal points, an approach which is taken by the Nagoya Protocol in place of mandatory disclosure requirement, is not yet established in Ethiopia. Therefore, our government and relevant stakeholders should work towards the establishment of a national focal point.

In case of research by both foreign and domestic institutions in relation to genetic resources; a risky approach of controlling after allowing is followed by the proclamation. However, it is better to make all the possible assessments before things are out of hand. In doing so; to require the submission of research proposals in advance is a wise move especially to assess the possible damage that the research may cause to the environment and genetic diversity.

Bibliography

Books

B. Claude and E. John, <u>Biotechnology and the Patent System: Balancing Innovation and Property Rights</u>, (2007), AEI Press, Washington D.C.

C. Jonathan, <u>The Protection of Biodiversity and Traditional Knowledge in International Law of Intellectual Property</u>, (2010), Cambridge University Press, New York

Gehl P., <u>Regulation Bio-pirospescting: Institutions for Drug Research, Access and Benefit-Sharing</u>, (2009) United Nations Press, USA,

M. Ikechi, <u>Global Bio-piracy: Patents, Plants, and Indigenous Knowledge</u> (2006), University of British Colombia Press, Columbia,

P. Oldham, <u>Global Status and Trends in Intellectual Property Claims: Genomics, Proteomics and Biotechnology</u> (2004), UNEP/CBD/WG-ABS/3/INF/4

Rao R. V., et al, <u>Genetic diversity and conservation and utilization of plant genetic resources</u>, (2002), Kluwer Acadamic Publisher, Netherlands,

Rimmer M., <u>Intellectual Property and Biotechnology</u> (2007), Edward Elgar Publishing Limited, UK

Shiva V., <u>Bio-piracy: The plunder of Nature and Knowledge</u>, (1997), South End Press, Brookline/USA,

Shiva V., <u>Protect or Plunder? , Understanding Intellectual Property Rights</u>,(2001) , Penguin Book India Ltd., India,

T. Geoff and R. Tasmin (ed.), <u>A Guide to International Negotiations and Rules on Intellectual Property, Biodiversity and Food Security</u>, (2008), Internal Development Research Center, Earthscan publisher

T. Toshiko (ed.), <u>Patent Law and Theory, A Handbook of Contemporary</u>

Research (2008), Edward Elgar Publishing Limited, UK,

Tansey G. and Rajotte T. (eds.), The Future Control of Food: A Guide to International Negotiations and Rules on Intellectual Property, Biodiversity and Food Security (2008), Earthscan publishing , UK

Journals and Articles

Bavikatte K. et al, "Towards a People's History of the Law: Biocultural Jurisprudence and the Nagoya Protocol on Access and Benefit Sharing", Law, Environment and Development Journal vol. 7/1 (2011), available at http://www.lead-journal.org/content/11035.pdf

C. Rosemary, "The Recognition of Indigenous Peoples' and Community Traditional Knowledge in International Law", Thomas Law Review, vol. 14, (2001)

Chege E. K. et al, "The Nagoya Protocol on Access to Genetic Resources and Benefit Sharing: What is New and what are the Implications for Provider and User Countries and the Scientific Community?", Law, Environment and Development Journal , vol. 6/3, (2010),

David C.* "Traditional and Modern-Day Bio-piracy: Redefining the Bio-piracy Debate", J.ENVTL. LAW AND LITIGATION, [Vol. 19(2)], (2004),

Joseph* R., "International Regime on Access and Benefit Sharing: Where Are We Now?" Asian Biotechnology and Development Review, Vol. 12 No. 3, (2010), Available at: http://ssrn.com/abstract=1754351

M. Ricolfi, "Biotechnology, Patents and Epistemic Approaches" Journal of Biolaw &Business, (2002), Special Supplement,

Margo A et al, "Patent First, Ask Question Later: Morality and Biotechnology in Patent Law", Mary Law Review, Issue 2 Volume 45 Article 3, (2003) Parasad K. et al, Access and Benefit Sharing from Genetic Resources, Available at http//: www.icimod.org/abs , Accessed on [11/14/2012]

Rowland A. et al, Piper Patents and Biotechnology: Issues Around the Patenting of Life Forms, An article

Smagadi A., "National Measures on Access to Genetic Resources and Benefit Sharing, The Case of Philippines", LEAD Journal, vol. 1/1,(2005), Available http://www.lead-journal.org/content/05050.pdf

Vaish V. et al, "Is there a Need to 'Substantially Modify' the Terms of the TRIPS Agreement?", Journal of Intellectual Property Rights, Vol. 17, (2012), Hyderabad India

Working Papers, Reports, Documents and Others

Afreen Sh., et al, Bio-prospecting: Promoting and Regulating Access to Genetic Resources and Benefit Sharing, (2008), kalkota india, Indian Institute of Management Calcutta Working Paper Series WPS No. 631, Cabrera J. et al., Overview of National and Regional Measures on Access to Genetic Resources and Benefit Sharing: Challenges and Opportunities in Implementing the Nagoya Protocol, (2nd ed., 2012),

Christiane et al, Intellectual Property Rights on Genetic Resources and The Fight against Poverty, 2011, Belgium, European Parliament's Committee on Development, Available at http://www.europarl.europa.eu/activities/committees/studies.do?language=E, Accessed on [October, 15/2012],

Ethiopian Flora Network, Available at http://www.Ibc.gov.et

Genetic Resources Conservation Program Annual Report, Report No. 1, University of California Genetic Resources Conservation Program, Available on http://grcp.ucdavis.edu/publications/doc1/R1Body.pdf, Accessed on [December 17/2012]

Gizachew Sileshi, The Ethiopian Legal Regime on Plant Variety Protection: Assessment of Its Compatibility with TRIPs Agreement, Implications and the Way Forward, LL.M Thesis, AAU, Law Faculty,(2010), (Unpublished),

H. Chris, Biodiversity, Bio-piracy and Benefits: What allegations of Bio-piracy tell us about Intellectual Property (unpublished) Jim Ch., Bio-prospect Theory, Available on http://poseidon01.ssrn.com/delivery.php?IDSSRnpdf, Accessed on [November 16/2012]

Koutouki K., The Nagoya Protocol: Status of Indigenous and Local communities, Legal Aspects of Sustainable Natural Resources, Legal working Paper Series, 2011, Available on http://cisdl.org/public/docs/legal/The%20Nagoya%20Protocol%20%20 Status%20of%20Indiginous%20and%20Local%20Communities.pdf, Accessed on [November 19/2012]

Mafuratidze R., Critical Review of the Nagoya Protocol on Access & Benefit Sharing: Analysis of its Provisions against the African Model Law and Possibilities for its Implementation at National Level, Available on http://www.ctdt.co.zw/attachments/079_NAGOYA%20PROTOCOL.pdf, Accessed on [December, 12/12]

Mallot H., Fair shares or bio-piracy? Developing ethical criteria for the fair and equitable sharing of benefits from crop genetic resources, (2010), Dissertation (unpublished), Munich, National Biodiversity Strategy and Action Plan, Government of the Federal Democratic Republic of Ethiopia, Institute of Biodiversity of Conservation, December 2005, Available at http://www.cbd.int/doc/world/et/et-nbsap-01-en.pdf, Accessed on [November 27/2012],

Nega Miherete, The Interface between Access to Genetic Resources, Benefit Sharing and Intellectual Property Right Laws in Ethiopia: Analysis of their Synergies, (2010), A Thesis for the Partial Fulfillment of LL.M., Addis Ababa University, Nijar G., "Technical Brie: The Nagoya Protocol on Access and Benefit-Sharing of Genetic Resources: analysis and implementation options for developing countries", South Centre, Research Paper, vol. no. 36, (2010), IUCN

P. Pan, Bio-prospecting: Issues and Policy Considerations (2006), Honolulu, Legislative Reference Bureau

Scutt H., Bio-piracy: A Defense, Intellectual Property Dissertation, (unpublished),

The Crucible Group, People, Plants, and Patents; The Impact of Intellectual Property on Trade, Plant, Biodiversity, and Rural Society, (1994) , International Development Research Centre, Canada,

The TRIPS-CBD Issue in the WTO: A South Asian Perspective, Available on **http://cutsgrc.org/pdf/CUTS_GRC_Note_on_TRIPS-CBD_Issues**, Accessed on [November 16, 2012]

What Comes After Nagoya? Addressing Developing Country Needs in Intellectual Property Rights and Bio-diversity, UNCTAD & ICTSD side event, a report, 2011, Available at **http://ictsd.org/downloads/2011/05/ictsd-unctad-what-comes-after-nagoya-report.pdf**, Accessed on [November, 22/2012]

National and International Legal Instruments

Agreement on Trade-Related Aspects of Intellectual Property Rights, Annex 1C of the Marrakesh Agreements, Morocco, 15 April 1994

Council of Ministers Regulation to Provide for: Access to Genetic Resources and Community Knowledge and Community Rights, Reg. No. 169/2009 Fed.

130

Neg.Gaz., 15th year No.67,

Nagoya Protocol on Access to Genetic Resources and the Fair and Equitable Sharing of Benefits Arising from their Utilization to the Convention on Biological Diversity, Secretariat of the Convention on Biological Diversity, UN

Proclamation Concerning Inventions, Minor Inventions and Industrial Designs, Proclamation NO.123/1995, Negarte Gazeta,54 The Year,no.25,

Proclamation to Provide for Access to Genetic Resources and Community Knowledge and Community Rights, Proclamation No.482/2006, Fed. Neg Gaz, year 13th, No. 13,

The Bonn Guideline

Interviews

Gemedo Dale (Ph.D.), Director of the Institute of Biodiversity and Conservation, interviewed in January, 2013

Tamire Haile, Legal Study and Dissemination Senior Expert, interviewed in May, 2013

Birhanu Adelo, Director General of Intellectual Property Office, interviewed in May, 2013

Websites

<http//: www. docsonline.wto.org>

<http//: www. ebookbrowse.com>

<http//: www. en.bookfin.org>

<http//: www. gigapedia.org>

<http//: www. henoline.org>

<http//: www.Ibc.org .et >

<http//: www. jstore.org>

<http//: www. ssrn.com>

<http//: www. wipo.int>

<http//: www. wipo.org>

<http//: www. wto.org

Annex 1

Agreement on access to, and benefit sharing from, ------------------ genetic resource

BETWEEN

THE INSTITUTE OF BIODIVERSITY CONSERVATION OF THE FEDERAL DEMOCRATIC REPUBLIC OF ETHIOPIA

AND

Signed for the provider   Signed for the company

-------------------------------------   ----------------------------------

------------------------------------ -----   ----------------------------------

Signature ----------------------   Signature -------------------------

Date ----------------------------   Date -------------------------------

Witnesses

Date --------------------------

Addis Ababa

1. Parties

The agreement is signed between:

The Institute of Biodiversity Conservation. Whose address is Yeka Sub city, Kebele 08 P.O. Box 30726; Telephone: 251-1-627504/612244, Fax: 251-1-627730/613722; E-mail:info@ibc.gov.et,Addis Ababa ,Ethiopia, hereafter referred to as the "provider"

And

--------------------------, Whose registered address is ------------sub city: ------ Kebele:----------

P.O. Box 18898 Tel 251 11 8611748, E.mail:-----------------------

City---------------, Country; Hereafter referred to as the **"Company"**

134

The provider and company shall hereinafter be jointly referred to as the "parties" and singularly or in the alternative be referred to as the 'party'

2. Preamble

Whereas, Ethiopia has immense biodiversity with actual or potential value and intends to share benefits arising out of the utilization of this resource by allowing access to the company;

Whereas, the company intends to ---------------------------- for processing ------ -- products;

One of the principal raw materials for the company is the species of ------------ known under its Scientific name --------------------- which is known to be available in the Ethiopian ---------------------------- (Ecosystem)

The provider has agreed to allow accessing the genetic resource/biological resource to the company to ---------------------- (harvesting, collecting, and processing etc.) from the areas stated below for valuable consideration; Therefore, the parties have agreed as follows:

3. The scope of access and obligations of the parties

3.1.   The provider agrees that the **Company** accesses and uses the above stated genetic resource/biological resource from the areas of ------------------------ ---to the amount not greater than ……..tons per month through the time of contract.

3.2.   Under this **agreement,** the **Company** is permitted to use the above stated genetic resource/biological resource only for the purpose of developing ---- ------------------ products.

3.3.   The **company** cannot use the genetic resource/biological resource for any other purposes whatsoever unless explicit written permit is given by the **Provider.**

3.4.   The **Provider** shall not grant to other parties access to the genetic resource/biological resource in the same area for the same product with the **company** unless it secures the consent of the **Company.**

3.5.   The company shall have the right to use the --------------- in a sustainable manner to achieve the intended purpose. And it shall take the necessary measures to ensure the sustainability and not to over exploit the genetic resource/biological resource. The provider shall issue all such documents, approvals, sanctions, and letters/permits as are required for the said purpose.

3.6.   The provider shall not be liable for any loss caused to company if the ---------- is not available due to force majeure in the said area.

3.7.   The **Company** is not permitted to access the traditional knowledge of Ethiopian communities on the conservation, cultivation and use of the genetic resource/biological resource. Therefore, the **Company** shall not claim any rights over, nor make commercial benefit out of, such traditional knowledge unless explicit written **agreement** is given to it by the **provider.**

3.8.   The **Company** shall assist in identifying and bringing to court infringers upon the rights of Ethiopia over the genetic resource/biological resource.

3.9   The Company shall respect the laws of the country, particularly those relating to sanitary control, biosafety and protection of the environment; and respect the cultural practices, traditional values and customs of local communities.

3.10   Furthermore, the company has obligations stated under the access to genetic resources and community knowledge, and community rights proclamation no.482/2006

4. Intellectual property ownership

4.1. The Company shall neither claim nor obtain intellectual property rights over the genetic resource/biological resource or any parts of the genetic resource/biological resource.

4.2. Any inventions based on the genetic resource/biological resource or parts thereof shall be jointly owned by both company and the provider.

5. Transfer to third parties

The **Company** shall not transfer this genetic resource/biological resource or any component of the genetic resource/biological resource to third parties without first having explicit written consent from the **provider.**

6. Effect of the agreement

6.1. The **agreement** shall not affect the sovereign rights of Ethiopia over the genetic resources/biological resource and the provider shall always retain the authority to grant other parties access to any genetic resources/biological resources of the same type save as the conditions stated under Art. 3.4 of this agreement.

6.2. The agreement shall be implemented in conformity with similar agreements that the provider may make in the future in a manner that does not substantially affect the interest of the company.

7. Benefit sharing

The **Company** has agreed to share the following monetary and non-monetary benefits that arise out of the utilization of the genetic resources/biological resources.

7.1. Monetary benefits

7.1.1.   The Company agrees to pay to the **provider** a lump sum equal to the amount ......% of net profit after the taxes. This payment shall be made immediately after the publication of the annual account of the **Company.**

7.1.2.   The **Company** agrees to pay to the provider annually a royalty of ...% of the net profit of the company.

7.1.3.   The Company agrees to pay the provider annually a license fee equal to .....USD.

7.1.4.   The company shall pay to the provider .....USD each year as upfront payment.

7.2.   Non-monetary benefits

7.2.1.   The **Company** agrees to involve Ethiopian scientists in the research it will undertake. The kinds of research on which Ethiopian scientists will participate and the mode of participation shall be specified by mutual agreement of the parties in the research plan of the **Company.** As appropriate the **Company** will contract out research to Ethiopian research institutions.

7.2.2.   The company agreed to share with the provider the results of research it will undertake on the genetic resource/biological resource. Accordingly, the company shall share with the provider the knowledge or technologies it may generate using this genetic resource/biological resource except where it constitutes undisclosed information to the company according to article 39 of the agreement on Trade-related Aspect of Intellectual property rights of the World Trade Organization.

7.2.3.   The company shall give training by inviting expertise for concerned institutions and local communities to enhance local skills in genetic resources/biological resource conservation, evaluation, development, propagation and use at least once in a year through the time of contract.

8. Ownership and confidentiality

8.1.   Results of any joint research conducted on the genetic resource/biological resource shall be owned by both parties and shall be released only upon written consent of both parties. Information that is identified by either party as confidential shall be kept as such by both parties.

8.2.   No party shall assign his rights, benefits, or obligations under this agreement to any third party without the written consent of the other party.

8.3.   Each of the parties shall at all times respect the confidentiality under this agreement and any information related to the other that it comes across or is disclosed to it including the know-how, manufacturing processes etc. And none of the parties shall give or disclose any such information to any third party without the prior written approval of the party to whom such information belongs.

9. Amendment

9.1.   Any provision of the agreement may be amended by the request of either party provided that the other party agreed the same.

9.2.   The amendments made as per Art. 9.1 shall make the integral part of the agreement.

10. Duration of the agreement

The **agreement** shall remain in force for a period of ....years. The parties may renegotiate the **agreement** at the end of that period.

11. Penalty

A party that breaches the terms of this agreement shall pay to the aggrieved party a penalty of .....USD if asked to do so by the aggrieved party.

12. Termination

12.1.   If one of the parties repeatedly fails to fulfill or violates its obligations under this **agreement,** then the aggrieved party may terminate the **agreement** upon 30 days' notice given in writing to the other party after going through the procedures under article 13 of the agreement.

12.2   The agreement shall also terminate upon court declaration of bankruptcy.

12.2. The agreement may terminate upon mutual agreement of both parties.

12.3.   The termination of this agreement shall not affect the rights and obligations that were due to accrue to either party prior to the effective date of termination.

12.4.   Starting with the day of termination of the agreement, the Company shall stop using the genetic resources/biological resources.

13. Dispute settlement

13.1.   If any dispute arises in connection with the interpretation or application of this agreement, both parties shall seek solution by negotiation. If the dispute cannot be resolved by negotiation, it shall be submitted to an arbitration body in accordance with the procedure laid down in part I to Annex II of the convention on biological Diversity.

13.2.   For the purpose of Art. 13.1, the word "party" in part I of Annex II of the Convention on Biological Diversity shall mean **"Provider"** and **Company"**.

13.3.   Either party who is aggrieved with the decisions of arbitrator may appeal to Ethiopian court or appropriate International court of law.

13.4.   If either of the party fails to comply with the award of the arbitral tribunal without appealing the case to ordinary court, the aggrieved party may, in accordance with paragraph 16 (d) (iv) of the Annex to section A of Decision Vi/24 of the 6th conference of the parties of the Convention on Biological Diversity, UNEP/CBD/COP/6/20, the Hague, 7-19 April 2002, ask the government of the Federal Democratic Republic of Ethiopia or the Government of ------------- to enforce the award given by the arbitral tribunal.

14. Guarantee

Each year, the Company shall pay USD....... ( ) in advance from which the requests by the provider for payment will be subtracted.

15. Applicable laws

15.1.   Access to genetic resources and community knowledge, and community rights proclamation no.482/2006 and other relevant Ethiopian laws.

15.2.   The Convention on Biological Diversity (CBD) and the relevant decisions, guidelines and laws that emanate from it.

15.3.   The CBD and the decisions, guidelines or laws that emanate from it shall prevail over the international union for the protection of new varieties of plants ("UPOV Convention") in cases on which the two do not agree.

16. Language of communication

Any communication between the parties including reports, minutes, records, instructions, notices, advice, correspondence or any other communication required under this agreement shall be made in English.

17. Monitoring and follow-up

17.1.   The provider shall have the right to ascertain the sustainability of the genetic resource/biological resource at any time.

17.2.   The Company shall submit to the provider annual research and financial Reports.

17.3.   The provider has the right to review at any moment, through an independent accountant if it so wishes, the book keeping as well as the relevant administrative details of the items covered by this agreement.

17.4.   Meetings between the two parties will be held as required to exchange information.

18. Entry in to force

The agreement shall enter into force from the Date of signature by the contracting Parties.

CPSIA information can be obtained
at www.ICGtesting.com
Printed in the USA
LVHW031030230323
742388LV00006B/43

9 783659 662294